CHRISTIAN M⟩   ⟩GE

CHRISTIAN MARRIAGE

*from basic principles
to transformed relationships*

D. M. Lloyd-Jones

THE BANNER OF TRUTH TRUST

THE BANNER OF TRUTH TRUST

3 Murrayfield Road, Edinburgh EH12 6EL, UK
P.O. Box 621, Carlisle, PA 17013, USA

*

© Lady Catherwood & Mrs Ann Beatt 2012

First published 1973 in *Life in the Spirit,*
Volume 6 of the Ephesians Series by
D. M. Lloyd-Jones

First published in this form 2012

ISBN: 978 1 84871 124 2

Typeset in 11/14 pt Sabon Oldstyle Figures at
The Banner of Truth Trust, Edinburgh

Printed in the U.S.A. by
Versa Press, Inc.,
East Peoria, IL

Contents

Publisher's Introduction

The eleven sermons in this volume were originally preached in Westminster Chapel on Sunday mornings as part of a lengthy series of expositions of Ephesians and have already appeared in print.[1] The way in which Dr Lloyd-Jones, following the Apostle Paul, deals with the marriage relationship is extremely important. He insists that these practical matters cannot be rightly understood apart from the profound truths of the Christian faith to which Paul relates them. To attempt to deal with Christian practice in isolation from Christian doctrine is to tread a dangerous path. In Dr Lloyd-Jones' view, the only Christianity powerful enough to penetrate and change society is that which is derived from the work of the Spirit of God.

In an age which has seen an almost total collapse of marriage, when, in many places, most marriages end in divorce with children

---

[1] The complete series is published by the Trust in eight volumes. The sermons in this book are taken from the sixth volume, *Life in the Spirit* (*Eph.* 5:18-6:9), ISBN: 978 0 85151 194 5, 372 pp., clothbound.

being raised in 'broken homes', Christian marriages can present a powerful witness to the supernatural realities which have entered the life of the world through the gospel of Christ. In this way they can point beyond merely practical matters to the profoundest truths of human existence.

The present situation, then, may be seen as giving Christians, and especially Christian marriages, a valuable opportunity to bear witness to the truth of the gospel. These sermons will afford considerable help in grasping this opportunity.

THE PUBLISHER
January 2012

Christian Marriage

Wives, submit yourselves unto your own husbands, as unto the Lord. ²³ For the husband is the head of the wife, even as Christ is the head of the church: and he is the saviour of the body. ²⁴ Therefore as the church is subject unto Christ, so let the wives be to their own husbands in every thing. ²⁵ Husbands, love your wives, even as Christ also loved the church, and gave himself for it; ²⁶ That he might sanctify and cleanse it with the washing of water by the word, ²⁷ That he might present it to himself a glorious church, not having spot, or wrinkle, or any such thing; but that it should be holy and without blemish. ²⁸ So ought men to love their wives as their own bodies. He that loveth his wife loveth himself. ²⁹ For no man ever yet hated his own flesh; but nourisheth and cherisheth it, even as the Lord the church: ³⁰ For we are members of his body, of his flesh, and of his bones. ³¹ For this cause shall a man leave his father and mother, and shall be joined unto his wife, and they two shall be one flesh. ³² This is a great mystery: but I speak concerning Christ and the church. ³³ Nevertheless let every one of you in particular so love his wife even as himself; and the wife see that she reverence her husband.

EPHESIANS 5:22-33

1. Basic Principles

Ephesians 5:22-33

WE COME NOW TO WHAT I have been describing as the practical application of the principle which the apostle laid down in the twenty-first verse, 'Submitting yourselves one to another in the fear of Christ'. There was the general principle, and now, as is his invariable custom, he comes to its particular application.

There can be no question at all that that is what the apostle is doing. We can prove it in three different ways. The first is, the word 'submit' which is found in the Authorized or King James Version, and also in other versions. 'Wives, submit yourselves unto your own husbands'. Actually in the original the word 'submit' is not there at all, it is just 'Wives, unto your own husbands, as unto the Lord'. How do we explain the omission of the word? It means that the apostle is carrying over the injunction about 'submitting' from verse 21 into verse 22. The very fact that the word is not actually repeated is therefore a proof that verse 22 is a continuation of verse 21, and that he is still dealing with the same theme, the general principle of submission. He knows that that will be in the minds of his readers, and therefore he says: 'Wives (in this matter of submission) unto your own husbands'. So the mere absence of the word 'submit' in the original is a proof in and of itself that that is what the apostle is doing here.

But there is a second proof. It is found in the fact that he mentions the wives before the husbands. That is not accidental; neither is it done merely out of politeness or on the principle of 'ladies first'. The Bible never does that. The Bible, as we shall see, and as the apostle expounds, invariably uses the other order. Indeed the law of the land does so, and we all do so in general parlance. We do not say Mrs and Mr So-and-so; we say Mr and Mrs—, and so on. So when the apostle puts the wives first in his consideration of the relationship of husbands and wives he has a very good reason for doing so. The reason is that he is particularly concerned about this question of submission—'submitting'. That is the principle which he has outlined in verse 21. Now in the married relationship the aspect of submission, as he shows, applies particularly to the wives. There is another aspect that applies to the husbands—and he deals with that, because his statement is a full one and a balanced one—but as he is primarily concerned about the question of submission, he inevitably and quite naturally puts the wives first. So there we have a second proof of the claim that what we are dealing with here is an outworking of the general principle laid down in verse 21.

Another, and a third, argument for this is, that he uses the expression 'unto your own husbands'. Note the emphasis, 'Wives, submit yourselves unto your own husbands'. In verse 21 he has laid down the general principle of submission on the part of all Christians to others—'Submitting yourselves one to another'. The argument, then, is this: If you do that in general, if you do that to everybody as it were, how much more so should wives do it to their own husbands in this peculiar relationship which has been defined so adequately in the Old Testament.

I am taking the trouble to emphasize this, because if we are not clear that verse 21 really is the controlling principle, we cannot possibly understand his detailed teaching correctly. Having cleared that point, let us now proceed.

Before we come to this vital and most important subject— especially so in these present days—it is most important that we should first of all look at the apostle's statement in general. Let us observe his method. I have many reasons for doing this. What the apostle does here we shall find him doing also in the case of 'children and parents' and 'servants and masters'. You notice the order in each case. The children come before the parents. Why? Because he is concerned about submission. Children do not come before parents; but in this matter they do, because it is a question of submission. The servants come before the masters, again for the same reason. I am arguing that when we study a portion of Scripture such as this—and as I have said, I am concerned at the moment to treat the matter in general—we shall find that the apostle employs his customary method; and if we succeed in grasping his method in one particular instance we shall find a key to the understanding of his other writings. Not only that; if we study exactly how the apostle deals with any one problem, if we really have discovered his method, then when we are confronted by a problem we shall find that all we need to do is to apply the method, and as we apply the method we shall be able to discover the answer. What we are doing then, primarily at the moment, is to study the apostle's method. Having done that we shall come to the particular subject with which he is dealing.

There are certain things which stand out very clearly in this particular paragraph which illustrate the apostle's method. Here is the first: The fact that we have become Christians does not mean that we shall be automatically right in all we think and in all we do. There are some people who seem to think that that is the case. The moment a man becomes a Christian, according to them, everything is perfectly plain and clear. Evangelists are often responsible for that, because in their anxiety to get results, they make extravagant statements, and they thereby leave many, many problems for pastors and teachers. The impression is given that you enter into some magical atmosphere; nothing is the same, everything is different, no problems, no difficulties! All you have to do is to take your decision, and the story will be, 'they all lived happily ever afterwards'—there will never be any problem or difficulty. Of course that is quite wrong. If that were true there would never have been a single epistle in the New Testament. The fact that we have become Christians, that the basic matter of our relationship to God has been put right, does not mean that we are now automatically right everywhere in all we think, and in all we say and do. The very paragraph we are looking at is proof, in and of itself, that we need instruction about particular matters.

The second principle of this: Not only is it true, as I have been saying, that the Christian is not automatically right about everything, because he is a Christian; we can even say that the fact that a man has become a Christian will probably raise for him new problems which he has never had to confront before. Or if it does not do that, it will certainly present to him problems that he has never faced before in this way. He now sees situations as he has never seen them before. Whereas he did not really think before, he is now compelled to think. And the moment he thinks, and because he thinks, he is confronted by new problems.

This was very much the case in the early church. It worked like this. Take the case of a wife. A husband and wife had been living together as pagans. Neither being Christians, they lived their married life as pagans did at that time. We shall have to refer to that later. But now the wife becomes converted and becomes a Christian. The temptation that immediately confronted such a wife was to say, 'Well now of course I am free. I understand things as I never understood them before. The gospel has told me that "there is neither barbarian, Scythian, male nor female, bond nor free." Therefore I do not continue to live now as I used to do. I have an understanding which my husband has not got'. The danger was for the wife to misinterpret her new life in such a way as to upset the marriage relationship. It was the same with children and parents, and it still tends to be the same. Very often when children are converted, and their parents are not, and have an understanding which their parents have not got, they misinterpret the new situation, and are led by the devil to misuse and abuse it. So in the end they are to be found breaking the commandment of God which tells the children to honour their parents. Thus, almost inevitably, with the enlightenment that comes with Christianity, new problems arise which had never to be faced before. So we gather from this passage that the great change which takes place in regeneration has a tendency to raise new problems. The result is that we have to think very carefully, to discover exactly what is right in this new life, and how we are to apply this new teaching to the new situation in which we find ourselves.

The third principle is this: Christianity has something to say about the whole of our life. There is no aspect of life which it does not consider, and which it does not govern. There must be no compartments in our Christian life. Very often, as you know, there are. The danger to these early Christians was, that these persons—husband and wife, or children or parents—on being converted, and becoming Christians, should say to themselves, as it were: 'Well of course, this is something that appertains to my religious life only, to the element of worship in my life; it has nothing to do with my marriage, it has nothing to do with my work, it has nothing to do with my relationship with my parents—and so on'. Now that is quite wrong according to this teaching. There is nothing so wrong and nothing so fatal, as to be living a life in compartments. Sunday morning comes and I say, 'Ah, I am a religious man'. So I take up my religious bag. Then Monday morning comes and I say to myself, 'I am now a businessman, or something else', and I take up another bag. So I am living my life in compartments; and it is difficult to tell on Monday that I am a Christian at all. Of course I showed it on Sunday when I went to a place of worship. This conception is entirely wrong. The Christian life is a whole;

the Christian faith has something to say about every realm and department of life.

Every one of these points is most important and could be greatly elaborated. There are those who say—and up to a certain point I am prepared to agree with them—that the present state of our churches, and of Christianity, is very largely due to the fact that many of our Victorian grandfathers were excessively guilty of the particular failure to realize that Christianity governs the whole of a man's life, and not only a part of it. Many of them were very religious people; some of them had prayers in their works or in their office in the morning, and then, having had the prayers, they became hard and grasping and unkind and unfair and legalistic. Undoubtedly they antagonized many against the Christian faith, because, so often, there was this kind of dichotomy, this failure to realize the wholeness of the Christian life, and that the Christian must never live a life in compartments. My Christianity must enter into my married life, into my relationship to parents, into my work, into everything I am, and into everything I do.

I come now to a fourth principle, which is again a most important one from the standpoint of doctrine and theology, and because of that, in ordinary life also. Christian teaching never contradicts or undoes fundamental biblical teaching with respect to life and living. I mean that there is no contradiction between the New Testament and the Old Testament. This needs to be emphasized at the present time because of the common attitude towards the Old Testament. People say glibly and superficially, 'Ah well, of course, we are not interested any longer in anything said in the Old Testament; we are New Testament people'. Some are foolish enough to say that they do not believe in the God of the Old Testament. They say, 'I believe in the God and Father of our Lord Jesus Christ'. Christian preachers, so-called, say from their pulpits, and it is applauded, that they do not believe in the God of Sinai, the

God of the Ten Commandments and the moral law. They dismiss the Old Testament teaching and say that we must be guided by the New Testament teaching only. Some of them even go further than that, and say that we are not even to be governed by the New Testament, because we know so much more by now.

There is this tendency to dismiss the whole of the biblical teaching. My answer is this: that the New Testament, the specifically Christian teaching, never contradicts, never sets aside the fundamental biblical teaching with regard to human relationships and the orders of life. I am referring, of course, to subjects like marriage, as we shall see here. The apostle's argument is based partly upon what is taught in the Old Testament, even in the Book of Genesis. It is the same with regard to the family, it is the same with all these fundamental orders in life. The fact that you become a Christian does not touch those at all. What it actually does is to supplement the Old Testament, to open it out, to give us a larger view of it, to help us to see the spirit behind the original injunction. But it never contradicts it.

This is a most important and vital principle. I am emphasizing it because as a pastor I have so often had to deal with it. People somehow get hold of the notion that, because they are new beings in Christ, the old fundamental principles no longer hold. The answer of the New Testament is that they do. Notice how the apostle quotes the Old Testament in all these instances, in order to show that the original teaching came from God, and that it must always be observed, however much it may be supplemented by this newer teaching.

Let us go on to the fifth principle. The New Testament always gives us reasons for its teaching. It always gives us arguments and there is nothing about it that I rejoice in so much as just that. The New Testament does not merely throw a number of rules and regulations at us and say, Now then, keep those. No!

It always explains, it always gives us an argument, it always gives us a reason. The kind of Christianity that simply imposes rules and regulations on people is a departure from the New Testament teaching; it is to treat us as children. Alas, there are such types of Christianity! It becomes a putting on of a uniform; and all Christians are 'like peas in a pod'. There they are, just going through their 'drill'. That is not Christianity! We should always know why we are behaving in this way; we should always understand the reason for it. We should be clear and happy about it; and therefore there should be no contradiction, there should be no 'kicking against the pricks', or working against the grain, or feeling that I have to do it but wish I had not to do it, but rather wishing to get as far away as I can from it. That is not Christianity. The Christian is a man who rejoices in the way he is living. He sees it clearly, he does not want anything else; it is inevitable, his mind is satisfied.

That is why I say that a man who is not a Christian does not know truly what it is to be a man. There is no teaching in the world that pays us such a compliment as this Word of God. It does not treat us as children and govern us by rules and regulations. It puts it to your reason, puts it to your understanding. That is true holiness teaching—not something you receive in a packet, not something that comes when you are more or less passive and unconscious. It is reasoning out the teaching, taking a principle and working it out, as the apostle does here. That is the New Testament method of holiness and sanctification. Thank God for it!

The sixth principle which I observe here is a most glorious one. How wonderful is this Scripture! To me it is amazing that as you look at this teaching you think at first, O well, that is of course merely teaching about marriage, husbands and wives. But then you begin to discover the treasures that are here; you go from room to room and it becomes more wonderful as you go on. Have you noticed, as you have read this passage, the intimate relationship between doctrine and practice? Doctrine and practice must never be separated, because each helps the other and each illustrates the other. There are certain respects in which this passage we are looking at is, to me, one of the most astounding in the whole of the Bible. I am not saying it is the greatest, but I say it is one of the most astounding. Here we are in this Epistle to the Ephesians in chapter 5, and towards the end of the chapter. What is happening in this part of the epistle? Well, says everybody, you are now in the practical section of the epistle. The great doctrinal section, of course, was chapters 1, 2 and 3. A little came into chapter 4, but now we have come down into the realm of practicalities and ordinary relationships, and most ordinary matters. Never was the apostle more practical than he is in your section—wives and husbands, children and parents, servants and masters—a purely practical section of his epistle. Yet you notice—and have not you always been amazed at this when you have read it for yourself, or when you have happened to be in a marriage service and this section of Scripture has been read—have not you been astounded and thrilled to the very marrow of your being as you find that the apostle in dealing with this most practical matter suddenly introduces us to the most exalted doctrine? In telling wives and husbands how to behave towards one another he introduces the doctrine of the nature of the church and the relationship of the church to Christ. Indeed I must go further. In this very section the apostle gives us his most exalted teaching of all about the nature of the church and the relationship of the church to Christ. This is something that we should never lose sight of. When you are reading this epistle be prepared for surprises. Do not say to yourself, 'Oh well, I need not pay much attention to this, this is of course practical and simple and direct'. Suddenly, when you are least expecting it, he will open a door, and there you will be confronted by the most magnificent and glorious doctrine you have ever met with in your life.

That leads me to make this practical comment. Beware of superficial analyses of Scripture. You know the type of person who says 'Chapter 1—this; chapter 2—that. All so perfect and neat and tidy!' If you try to do that with this chapter of the Epistle to the Ephesians you will find yourself bewildered, and your little scheme upset. Here, in this most practical of sections, Paul suddenly introduces this tremendous doctrine of the nature of the church, and the relationship of the church to the Lord Jesus Christ. But what we must bear in mind—because it comes out of all that—is that doctrine and practice are so intimately related that they cannot be separated. Anyone, therefore, who says, 'I am only interested in the practical', is really denying the essence of the Christian message. This great passage demonstrates that in a perfect manner.

Having said those six things, I say in the seventh place: Obviously in the light of all this, when you are confronted by any problem, never approach it directly, never start by considering the thing per se, in and of itself. That is what we all tend to do. How often have I found this in discussion groups and meetings! A question is put forward—a practical problem in somebody's daily life and living and I put it to the meeting. The tendency is for people to get up at once and to speak directly on the question, and to give their opinions on it. And for that reason, of course, they are generally wrong; because that is not the way to approach a problem.

The apostle does not approach this problem of husbands and wives, and wives and husbands directly, immediately per se, as if it were an isolated question. His method is this—you must always approach it indirectly. It is, once more, 'the strategy of the indirect approach'. When I am confronted by a particular question I must not immediately apply my mind directly to it. I must first ask the question, Is there any principle, is there any doctrine in the Scripture, that governs this kind of problem? In other words, before you begin to deal with the individual problem, as it were, that is in front of you, you say: Well, what family does he belong to? You might go even wider and say: What nation does he belong to? Get hold of a big classification, and having discovered the truth about the group or the class or the great company, you then proceed from that to apply the principle to that particular instance or example. That is what the apostle does here. He starts with the general and then comes to the particular.

I have often used the following illustration. Anyone who has ever done any chemistry and who has been asked to identify a substance will at once recognize the method. How does he proceed? He does the very thing I have just been saying. He starts with the most general tests, the big group tests. Thus he can exclude certain groups; and he narrows it down to one group. Then he has to divide it up into divisions, the subdivisions of the group; and then narrows it down and down and at last he comes to the particular individual substance. That is the apostle's method here as it is indeed his method everywhere. It is 'the strategy of the indirect approach', the movement from the general to the particular. Never jump at a problem, never tackle it in and of itself; get hold of the great principle or governing doctrine.

The last point I make is this, and again it is a very practical one. I deduce it from all that has gone before. Notice the spirit in which the apostle conducts the discussion. Here he is taking up the problem of the relationship of wives and husbands, and husbands and wives; but notice his method, notice the spirit in which he does it. This subject is one of the standing jokes of the world is it not? This is something that can always raise a laugh. The poorest comedian tries to make something of this when he has nothing else—marriage relationships, husbands and wives. I need not point out that the apostle does not handle it in this way. You cannot handle any Christian problem like that.

But there are other negatives also. Not only does he not handle it jocularly, flippantly and lightly, there is a complete absence of a partisan spirit here. There is nothing heated, nothing assertive, no standing for rights, no anxiety to prove that one is right and the other wrong. That is how matters are normally dealt with, is it not? And that is why there is so much trouble. The apostle evades all that, as I have been saying, by lifting it up and putting it into another context; and by doing that he avoids all these difficulties.

His method, positively, is this; it is the principle 'in the fear of Christ' that he has already laid down in verse 21: 'Submitting yourselves one to another in the fear of Christ'. Then he repeats it: 'Wives, submit yourselves unto your own husbands, as unto the Lord'. Before you begin to take your stand on the one side or on the other—and if you do, you are already doomed to failure because you are in a partisan spirit—he prevents all partisan spirit, he raises both immediately 'to the Lord'. Every subject that is discussed by Christians should be discussed in that way. A Christian who loses his or her temper in an argument should not speak. Whether you prove your point or not you have lost everything by losing your temper. It is 'in the Lord', 'in the fear of Christ'. Paul is talking about submission, and his point is that before we consider the merits of these two people, both of them must submit themselves unto the Lord, 'Submitting yourselves one to another in the fear of Christ'. And as both do that, you will have your argument 'on your knees'. What a difference that makes! If I may use a vulgarism, you must not get up on your hind legs; you must get down on your knees. If only we conducted these difficult matters upon our knees what a difference it would make!

This is not only true concerning the question of husbands and wives. Take the heat that is generated over the argument about pacificism, and the various other matters that are engaging people today—the heat, the partisan spirit, the animosity! The method, says the apostle, the spirit, is that we must do it always in submission to the Lord, with a desire to please him, with a readiness always to be taught and to be led by him and by his Word.

There, we have seen eight general principles which not only govern this particular matter but govern every problem that can ever arise in your Christian life. Having done that, let us go on to the particular matter. All I have been saying is illustrated to perfection in the apostle's treatment of the Christian view of marriage, the Christian teaching concerning marriage. But, once more, we must follow the method. Before we come to the details let us look at what he tells us in general about this.

The first big thing he tells us is, that the Christian view of marriage is a unique view; it is a view that is entirely different from every other view; it is a view that you only find in the Bible. How does the Christian view marriage? What is the teaching? Let me start again with a negative. The Christian's way of viewing marriage is not the way in which marriage is generally viewed by the vast majority of people. Have you ever thought of this? What if I asked you at this point to write an account of the Christian view of marriage. Have you ever done that? Shame on us who are Christians if we do not have a clear and well-defined view. Have we discovered the uniqueness of the Christian view, have we realized how it differs so essentially from the general view? What is that general view?

Unsavoury though it is, I must remind you of it. The common view of marriage is a purely physical one. It is something which is based almost exclusively on physical attraction, and the desire for physical gratification. It is a legalizing of physical attraction and physical gratification. So often it is nothing but that—hence the scandal of mounting divorce. The parties have not even thought about it, they have no view of marriage at all; they are governed entirely by instincts and impulses; it is all purely on the animal level, and never rises above it. There is no thought whatsoever about marriage in and of itself; it is but a legalizing of something that they are anxious to do.

Then there is a second common view which rises a little higher than the first. It is a little more intelligent than that because it regards marriage as a human arrangement and a human contrivance. Anthropology teaches us this, they say. There was no doubt a time, they say, when human beings were more or less like animals; they were promiscuous and behaved as animals behave. But as man began to develop, and to evolve, he began to realize that certain arrangements were necessary, that promiscuity led to confusion and to excess, and to a lot of trouble; so after a long process of agonizing and of development, and of experiment, and of trial and error, human nature in its wisdom, that is, civilization, came to the conclusion that it would be right and well and good that you should have monogamy—one man marrying one woman. It is a matter of social development—that is the teaching of anthropology. But the whole time it is something that man has discovered. As he passes Acts of Parliament to control traffic and parking and so on, so he has discovered a way of solving this problem of man and woman and their relationships to one another, and to children. It is something entirely on the human plane. That is probably the common assumption which is made by the vast majority of people. Alas, I find it at times even among Christian people!

Another characteristic of this view—and it arises because it has not a fundamentally correct view of marriage—is that the whole approach to marriage is one which almost expects trouble. That was very true of the pagan world. Husbands tended to tyrannize over their wives and to make slaves of them, and the wives acted deceitfully. The atmosphere was one of jealousy and antagonism, leading to strife and quarrelling of necessity. Instead of this common submission to the Lord, each one stood for his or her rights. Not a true partnership, but a kind of agreement that for certain purposes they were going to do certain things together; but actually there was an underlying bitterness and antagonism of spirit and sense of opposition.

Examine the commonly held view of marriage, and of the marriage state and relationship. You see it in the cartoons, you see it in the reports of the cases in the courts, you see it, I say again, in the popular jokes. Why should it be thus? How has this come to be so current? It is because of this completely wrong view of what marriage really means. Today the whole question has become aggravated because of the modern notions of equality between men and women resulting from the so-called feminist movement. This has aggravated the whole problem; and it makes the subject we are dealing with particularly urgent at the present time. There has been this modern movement of feminism which claims that men and women are equal in every respect, and that there should be no division or distinction at all, but complete equality. Now while, on the one hand, there are aspects of that teaching with which any Christian man, leave alone any sane intelligent man, must agree with the whole of his being, on the other hand, taking it in general, and as a principle, it goes against the plain teaching of the Scripture at this point. It is without any question the cause of much confusion, much trouble, and much damage, not only to the marriage state, but also to the family as a fundamental unit in life. The result is that discipline has gone, order has gone, and children are not given a chance. Why? Because their parents are not in the right relationship to one another; and the child is bewildered at seeing this competition, this conflict, where there should be unity. This modern feminist movement has tended to becloud the whole issue; and, alas! it seems even to be seeping into the thinking of many who call themselves evangelical, and who claim to believe in the Scripture as the infallible Word of God and our only authority.

We see at once here that that is not the Christian approach to marriage. The Christian view of marriage is governed entirely and solely by the teaching of the Scripture—the Old Testament and the New Testament, both. The apostle derives his argument from the Old Testament as well as from Christ. So a man who claims to be a Christian does not say, 'Now, well, what I think about marriage is this'. He says rather, 'What does the Bible say about marriage?' Thus, there is a complete difference at the very beginning—he 'submits' himself to the teaching of this book. He does not say, 'Of course by now we have developed and advanced so much. Women were virtually thought of as slaves even by the Apostle Paul, you know. He was so right on the atonement, but not on the subject of women!' The moment you say that, you no longer believe the Scriptures, and you have no right to say that you believe they are the infallible Word of God. No, the Christian says 'I know nothing apart from what the Scripture tells me'. So he submits to the Old Testament and to the New Testament. His whole life is to be governed on that principle—in the matter of thought as well as conduct.

Secondly, we discover that marriage is not a human contrivance or arrangement, but God's ordinance, something instituted by God, something that God in his infinite grace and kindness has appointed and ordained and prepared and established for men and women. It is of God and not of man. The teaching of the anthropologists is based on speculation and imagination; it is not true. The teaching of the Bible is the truth about this matter; it is God's contrivance and God's ordinance.

Thirdly, the terms of the relationship, as we shall find, are clearly and plainly stated.

Fourthly, marriage can only be fully understood as we understand the doctrine of the Lord Jesus Christ and the church. You notice that that is central; the apostle carries on the argument about Christ and the church right through the paragraph. In other words it comes to this; if we are not clear about the Lord Jesus Christ and the church, and the relationship of the church to him, we cannot understand marriage. It is impossible because it is only in the light of that doctrine that we really understand the doctrine concerning marriage.

I therefore draw these two deductions. It is only the Christian who truly understands and appreciates marriage. That is one of the wonderful results of being a Christian. Christianity not only deals with your soul, and your final salvation, your avoidance of hell and your going to heaven; Christianity touches the whole of your life while you are still in this world. I think I can say honestly that in my pastoral experience, there has been nothing more wonderful than to see the difference Christianity makes in the husband/wife relationship. Where there was a tendency to part and to drift from one another, and an antagonism and almost a bitterness and a hatred, the two people on becoming Christians have discovered one another for the first time. They have also discovered for the first time what marriage really is, though they may have been married for years. They now see what a beautiful and what a glorious thing it is. You cannot understand marriage unless you are a Christian.

May I venture to put it like this? In the light of all this, the wonder is, not that there are so many divorces, but that there are not many more. Is it not amazing and astounding that in the general absence of thought, and even with wrong thinking when they do begin to think, marriages hold even as they do? No man, no woman has a true conception of marriage who is not a Christian; but if we are Christians there should be no difficulty about knowing what marriage is, and what it means. There should be no argument, there should be no disputation. If you believe the doctrinal teaching the view of marriage is inevitable. Not only is it inevitable, you are very glad that it is inevitable. It is so wonderful, it is so glorious, it is so exalted. There is no difficulty, there is no haggling, there is no argument. You have submitted yourself to Christ; so has the other. And you have both submitted yourselves not only to one another, but to all the other members of the church, the community to which you belong. You are governed by a higher loyalty, by loyalty to him who did not consider his own rights and prerogatives, but who considered you only, and your desperate and appalling need. He humbled himself, laid aside his rights and prerogatives, and took upon him even the form of a servant, and even went to death, yea the death of the cross. Looking at him, and seeing how he came not only to save you from hell, but to give you life, and to give you life more abundantly, and to fill out your understanding of everything to his own glory—seeing that, you see marriage anew, you see everything anew. You do not object to the biblical teaching, you not only submit yourself to it, you rejoice in it, and you praise God for it.

There, then, is our introduction to the detailed teaching of the Apostle Paul in Ephesians chapter 5 with regard to Christian marriage. We can now go on to consider the teaching in detail.

2. The Order of Creation

Ephesians 5:22-24

WE NOW COME TO A MORE detailed consideration of the teaching of this passage, indeed the teaching of the New Testament and of the entire Bible with regard to marriage. We have looked at it in general, and have done so because of the way in which the apostle presents it to us; and it is essential that we should bear all that in mind.

The spirit in which we approach this matter is most important. Everything that is done in the realm of the church is different from what is done outside. The world in its debating societies debates the subject of marriage, and does so in a particular way and manner—two sides, for and against, the supporters and partisans. But that is not the way in which the church faces the problem; it does not face any problem like that. Here, we are confronted by the authority which we have in the Word. We are not concerned to express our own opinions; our one purpose is to understand the teaching of the Word. And we do so together—not one group and another, opposition and government as it were, defence and attack. We all come together in order to discover the teaching of the Holy Scripture; and we have seen that certain great principles are laid down so clearly that all this is at once lifted up to the level of Christian doctrine at its highest. We are confronted by some of the most profound teaching found anywhere in the Scriptures concerning the nature of the Christian church.

Having looked at those general principles we can now proceed to the particular application. You notice that the first thing is an injunction which is given to wives. You remember we saw that the wives are put before the husbands for one reason only, that the apostle is dealing with the question of submission. The principle is in verse 21: 'Submitting yourselves one to another in the fear of Christ'. In this matter of submission, he says, first of all, 'Wives, submit yourselves, or be subject to your own husbands, as unto the Lord'. The matter we have to consider is this 'submission' of wives to husbands. The apostle not only reminds them of that, but he tells them very plainly and clearly that it is their duty to do this—as it is the duty of all of us to submit ourselves one to another. This is a very special thing, he says, 'Wives, submit yourselves unto your own husbands'. This is still more obvious because they are their husbands, their own husbands, and because of the teaching with respect to the whole question of marriage. The big point, Paul says, that emerges here is this question of submission—that is what he is emphasizing. We must therefore look into this; and fortunately the apostle helps us to do so. It is not just an injunction thrown out at random.

Paul gives us first of all a great motive for this submission: 'Wives, submit yourselves unto your own husbands, *as unto the Lord*'. We must be clear about this phrase because it can be, and has been, misunderstood. It does not mean, 'Wives, submit yourselves unto your own husbands in exactly the same way as you submit yourselves unto the Lord'. It does not mean that, because that is going too far. The submission of every wife, and indeed of every Christian believer, male or female, to the Lord Jesus Christ is an absolute one. The apostle does not say that about the relationship of the wives to the husbands. We are all the bond-slaves of Jesus Christ, the 'slaves' of Christ; but a wife is never told to be the slave of her husband. Our relationship to the Lord is one of complete, entire, absolute submission. Wives are not exhorted to do that.

What, then, does it mean? It means: 'Wives, submit yourselves unto your own husbands because it is a part of your
duty to the Lord, because it is an expression of your submission to the Lord'. Or 'Wives, submit yourselves to your own
husbands; do it in this way, do it as a part of your submission
to the Lord'. In other words, you are not doing it only for the
husband, you are doing it primarily for the Lord himself. It is
a repetition of the general point made in verse 21, 'Submitting
yourselves one to another in the fear of Christ'. You do not
do it, in the last analysis, for the husband's sake; the ultimate
reason and motive does not rest there; the submission is 'unto
the Lord'. You are doing it for Christ's sake, you are doing it
because you know that he exhorts you to do it, because it is
well-pleasing in his sight that you should be doing it. It is a part
of your Christian behaviour, it is a part of your discipleship.
'Whether ye eat, or drink' says the apostle using the same sort
of argument in writing to the Corinthians in the First Epistle in
chapter 10, 'Whether ye eat, or drink, or whatsoever ye do, do
it as unto the Lord'. Everything we do is done for his sake, to
please him, because we know that he would have us do this.

Thus at the beginning the apostle lifts this matter up from
the realm of controversy and enables us to approach it in the
right spirit. If, he says, you are anxious to please the Lord
Jesus Christ, and to carry out his behests and his will, submit
yourselves unto your own husbands. There can be no more
compelling motive for any action than this; and every Christian
wife who is concerned above everything else to please the Lord
Jesus Christ, will find no difficulty in this paragraph; indeed
it will be her greatest delight to do what the apostle tells us
here. I would go further. Never, perhaps, have we as Christian
people had a greater opportunity of showing what Christianity
really means than precisely at this present time when the life
of the world is showing itself increasingly in its true colours.
Its life is becoming more and more chaotic in this matter of

the marriage relationship and in every other respect. Here is a glorious opportunity for us to show the difference it makes to be a Christian. So, Christian wives, says the apostle, you have a wonderful opportunity; you can show that you are no longer pagans, that you are no longer irreligious, that you no longer belong to the world. And these other people—living as they do, asserting their own rights, and displaying the arrogance which leads to all the chaos that characterizes life—when they look at you will see something so different that they will say, 'What is this? Why do you behave like this? What is the reason for it?' And your answer will not be 'Well, I just happen to be born like this', but 'I am behaving like this because it is the will of my Lord'. So you immediately get an opportunity for preaching and stating the gospel.

That is why the apostle exhorts them to this. The point of his entire exhortation—as we see in the whole of this chapter and most of the previous chapter—is that these Christian people are to show in every detail of their lives that once you become a Christian you are different in every respect. So this great characteristic of the Christian life can be displayed by the wives submitting themselves to their own husbands. That is the grand motive; and unless we are moved by it, and animated by it, no other argument will appeal to us. If we are not already submitted to the Lord Jesus Christ, and concerned about his name and his honour above everything else, all other arguments will leave us untouched. The apostle puts that first; and we have to put it first.

But having said that, Paul then goes on to give us particular reasons, additional reasons. Here again we note the wealth and the glory of the Scripture. There are two great subsidiary reasons, he says, why every Christian wife should submit herself to her own husband. The first is what we may call 'the order of creation'; the second, that this is something which belongs to the realm of the relationship of the church to the

Lord Jesus Christ. Both reasons are in the twenty-first verse: 'For [because]' — here is the first reason — 'the husband is the head of the wife'. The second reason is, 'even as Christ is the head of the church: and he is the saviour of the body'.

Look at the first reason. It is that this is a part of the order of creation, a part of God's ordinances, of God's decree, of God's will, of what God has stated with regard to this relationship between men and women. This is teaching which is to be found in various portions of Scripture. You find it first in the second chapter of Genesis right back at the creation; and you notice how the references in the New Testament all lead us back there. That is what I mean by saying that it belongs to the order of creation. Before you come to consider marriage from the specifically Christian standpoint you must go further back, because the New Testament sends you back. It sends you back to the Book of Genesis and to the whole question of creation. It also refers us to the question of the Fall. The account of that is found in the third chapter of Genesis. The crucial verse is the sixteenth verse, which tells us what God said to the woman as the result of her listening to Satan and his temptation, and her eating of the forbidden fruit. 'Unto the woman he said, I will greatly multiply thy sorrow and thy conception; in sorrow thou shalt bring forth children; and thy desire shall be to thy husband, and he shall rule over thee.' That is an addition to Genesis chapter 2, and we must pay careful attention to it.

In order to summarize the Scripture teaching concerning this most important matter of marriage and of the family, we may extract the principles that are put before us in these various portions of Scripture. Remember that we are dealing essentially with 'marriage' and not with the status of woman (or of all women) as such. Certainly we have to deduce from the Scriptures the teaching with regard to women in general, and such matters as the question of women entering the professions and so on. But I am not dealing with that, I am dealing only with the question of marriage. That is what the apostle does here; he is addressing wives. He is not addressing unmarried women at this point. There is teaching about that, but it does not come within our province here except indirectly.

The teaching is the following: First, you notice that the emphasis is put constantly upon the fact that the man was created first, not the woman. So there is a natural priority for man. The Scriptures also emphasize the fact that woman was made out of the man, taken out of the man, and meant to be a 'help' for man, a help for man that was 'meet' for him. None of the animals could supply that need. 'Adam gave names to all cattle, to the fowl of the air, and to every beast of the field; but for Adam there was not found an help meet for him.' And it was because there was no help meet for man amongst the animals, that woman was created.

That is the basic teaching, and notice that the apostles lay great stress upon it. Man was created first. But not only that; man was also made the lord of creation. It was to man that this authority was given over the brute and animal creation; it was man who was called upon to give them names. Here are indications that man was put into a position of leadership, lordship, and authority and power. He takes the decisions, he gives the rulings. That is the fundamental teaching with regard to this whole matter.

The Apostle Peter underlines all this in that significant phrase of his, where he tells the husbands to give honour to the wife 'as unto the weaker vessel' (*1 Pet.* 3:7). What does he mean by 'weaker vessel'? Clearly he means what is taught so plainly in the early chapters of Genesis, and, indeed, everywhere in the Bible. It means primarily this whole question of man's headship and leadership. Man, physically speaking, is naturally stronger than woman; he was made to be such, and he is such. I could enter into this in great detail. I could establish all this with extreme ease, not merely from the standpoint of anatomy, but still more from the standpoint of physiology. Woman was not meant to be as strong as man physically, nervously, and in many other aspects. She is constituted in a different manner; and when the apostle says that she is the 'weaker vessel' he is not speaking in any derogatory sense at all. He is simply saying that she is essentially different from man, and that man must ever bear that in mind. He must not treat the woman as if she were his equal in these respects. He must remember that she has been made differently, and that he is to respect her and to honour her, to guard and to protect her accordingly.

Here, then, is this basic fundamental teaching—the man is to be the head of the wife, and he is to be the head of the family. God made him in that way, endowed him with faculties and powers and propensities that enable him to fulfil this; and so made woman that she should be the 'complement' of man. Now the word 'complement' carries in itself the notion of submission; her main function is to make up a deficiency in the man. That is why these two become 'one flesh'; the woman is the complement of the man. But the emphasis, therefore, is this, that man is responsible not only for himself, but for his wife, and for his family in all ultimate matters. The wife is to help him, to support him, to aid him, and to do everything she can in order to enable him to function as the lord of creation, into which position God has placed him. She is brought into being in order to help man to perform that great and wonderful and glorious task. That is the basic teaching with regard to the relationship of husbands and wives as laid down in the very order of creation, the fundamental rules with regard to the life of man in this world.

But we must go further. That is how it was before the Fall. While man and woman were still perfect, while they were still in paradise without any sin, without any defect in them, that was how God ordained it. But unfortunately something happened—the Fall. Its importance is made very clear, especially by the Apostle Paul in the First Epistle to Timothy, in the second chapter, verses 11 to 15, at the end of the section. Notice that the apostle makes a great deal of the fact that it was the woman who was deceived and fell first, and not the man. So the Fall has made a further difference—Genesis 3:16 establishes that. Here it is again: 'Unto the woman he said, I will greatly multiply thy sorrow and thy conception'. From that one can but deduce that childbirth would probably have been painless had it not been for sin and the Fall. 'In sorrow thou shalt bring forth children.' But, for our purpose now—'thy desire shall be to thy husband, and he shall rule over thee'. Here is something additional. It not only reiterates the lordship, the leadership and the headship already established before the Fall; it underlines it—'he shall rule over thee'. There is a new element here; woman's subordination to man has been increased as the result of the Fall. Now it is arguable that God's edict was promulgated for this reason—that the very essence of the Fall, of what happened to Eve, was that Eve, being confronted by the insinuation and the suggestion of the devil, instead of doing what she should have done, what she had done hitherto, and been taught to do, namely, to go to Adam and to consult him about the question, took the decision upon herself, and put herself into the position of leadership. She dealt with the situation, and as the result of her dealing with the situation, instead of taking it to Adam, as she should have done, she fell. She involved him in the fall likewise, and so the whole human race fell. So that, in a sense, the original sin was that woman failed to realize her place and her position in the married relationship, usurped authority and power and position, and thereby brought calamity and chaos to pass. That is not only stated in Genesis 3:16, it forms the whole basis of the apostle's argument with regard to women taking authority, and teaching and preaching, in the First Epistle to Timothy, in the second chapter.

That is the teaching in its essence. But, at once, there is an objection, an objection that one reads and hears so frequently—and, alas, often from evangelical people who claim to believe the Scriptures as the infallible inspired Word of God. What one hears so often is this: 'Ah, but that is only the view of the Apostle Paul. He was obviously an anti-feminist, a man who held the view that was so commonly taken of women at that time'. It is emphasized that at that time woman was in a very debased position. Everybody throughout the world then held that view; woman was but 'goods' as it were, a slave. And as this was true even of the Jews, the apostle was just a typical rabbinical Jew. So runs the argument.

It is not surprising that people who do not believe the Scriptures as the Word of God say such things. They do not hesitate to say, not only that Paul was wrong, but that the Lord Jesus Christ was wrong. They are the authority; they know, they understand. I do not argue with such people; I simply say that I cannot have any discussion with them at all, because it is not merely a question of putting up my opinion against theirs. There is nothing else to say about it—it is not Christian at all. The Christian is a man who submits himself entirely to the biblical revelation; he knows nothing apart from this. So when we hear this argument, we not only bemoan it and regret it, we have to answer it, and we answer it in this way. To speak generally, it is perfectly true to say that the view of woman at the time of our Lord and of the Apostle Paul was debased. But it was not the Jews' view, for they had these Scriptures and believed them. And it most certainly was not the Apostle Paul's view. Have you noticed what he says in 1 Corinthians 11:11? His words run: 'Neither is the woman without the man, nor the man without the woman, in the Lord'. This great apostle gloried in the fact that in Christ Jesus there was neither barbarian nor Scythian, bond nor free, male nor female. It was a vital part of his preaching of the gospel to say: 'In this matter of salvation men and women are equal, and woman has an equal chance in salvation with man'. He gloried in that, and there is no man who speaks more delicately or more gloriously about womanhood, and of the true glory of womanhood, than the Apostle Paul. Further, notice that he does not limit himself to giving us an account of the duty of the wives towards the husband only, he always tells us about the duty of the husband to the wife also; and he shows that the Christian husband's view of womanhood, and of woman, and of his wife, is more exalted than anything the world has ever known. He puts everything into its right position. He always gives us the two sides.

But apart from all that, the apostle never puts these things forward as his own opinion; he always goes back to Genesis, and to the order of creation. He says, in effect, 'It is not my opinion, this is what God has laid down.' The apostle's only concern is that the truth of God should be known, and that what God ordained should be put constantly into practice. So this tendency to say that it is 'only Paul's opinion' is a denial of the Scripture. We must be quite clear about this. If you say you believe that the Bible is the infallible and inspired Word of God, then you must not speak in the world's way about the Apostle Paul; because when he writes he not only quotes the Scripture, he also writes as an inspired apostle. When he gives his own opinion he is always careful to say so, and if he does not say it is his own opinion, it is inspired. Remember how the Apostle Peter tells his readers to listen to the Apostle Paul. He says that some people wrest Paul's arguments and his writings to their own destruction 'even as they do also the other Scriptures' (2 *Pet.* 3:16). What Paul writes is Scripture; so the critics are not arguing with Paul, they are arguing with God, they are arguing with the Holy Ghost. At the same time they are putting themselves into the contradictory position of saying that they believe the Bible only as long as it does not contradict what they happen to believe as creatures of the twentieth century. That is a denial of a belief in the authority of the Scripture.

Having dealt with that foolish objection—and there is nothing that is more foolish than such talk—let me sum up the position again. Woman, according to this teaching, the wife, is given a certain status. To be subject to her husband does not mean that she is the slave of her husband, it does not mean that she is inferior to her husband as such—no, not for a moment! We shall see this still more clearly when we come to consider what the apostle says about the duty of the husband to the wife. What he is saying is that the woman is different, that she is the complement of the man. What he does prohibit is that woman should seek to be manly, that is, that a woman should seek to behave as a man, or that a woman should seek to usurp the place, the position, and the power which have been given to man by God himself. That is all he is saying. It is not slavery; he is exhorting his readers to realize what God has ordained. Therefore the wife should rejoice in her position. She has been made by God to help man to function as God's representative in this world. She is to be the home-maker, the mother, the helper of man, his comforter, the one to whom he can speak and look for comfort and encouragement—she is a help meet for man. Man realizes the truth about himself, she also realizes the truth about herself, and thus she complements him and aids him; and together they live to the glory of God and the Lord Jesus Christ.

An illustration may help at this point. The idea of leadership or headship stumbles certain people, because they seem to think that that of necessity carries the idea of an inherent and essential inferiority. But it is not so. This whole notion of the headship of the man, the husband, in the married relationship is comparable in many ways to that of troops to their leader. An army would be completely chaotic if each one had the right to decide what is going to be done next. As I have said previously, the moment a man joins the armed forces he is subjecting himself, he is saying that he is going to obey the command that comes down to him, no matter what he may think of it; it is his business to do so. He is granting this right of command to the one who is set above him; and though he may have his own ideas and opinions, he now foregoes them; he submits and he is in subjection.

Or, if you like, think of a number of men in a team playing football or cricket. The first thing they have to do is to appoint a captain. They are not all captains; if they were they would never win a match. The first thing they do is to appoint one amongst themselves as a captain. He may not even be the best player in the team, but they decide that on the whole he has the greatest gift of leadership. So they put him into the position of captain, and having done that they have to submit themselves to him. If they fail to do so, chaos has returned again.

Or imagine a committee being appointed to consider a subject. A number of men are appointed. The first thing they do is to appoint a chairman. Of course! Why? Because you must have some authority. You cannot transact business unless there is a chair to address, and you have to abide by the ruling of the chairman. Here again the question of inferiority does not come in. It simply means that in order to do this thing efficiently you must have a leader. Take a new House of Commons. The first thing they do is to appoint a Speaker; and the business of the Speaker is just to sit in the chair and exercise control, and to give his ruling. Again, it does not mean that he is the greatest man in the House of Commons, and that they are all inferior to him. No! In their wisdom, and because business cannot be transacted apart from this, they set someone in this position of authority. Now the Bible teaches that God has set man, the husband, in that position. So the apostle says to the wives, 'Wives, submit yourselves to your own husbands' for the reason that the husband has been appointed the head.

But a still greater argument is found in 1 Corinthians 11, where we are told that the man, the husband, is the head of the wife, that Christ is the head of the man, and that God is the head of Christ. This is an argument that cannot be disputed. In what sense is God the head of Christ? The answer is what we sometimes call the economic Trinity. The Father, Son and Holy Spirit are co-equal and co-eternal. How then can the Father (God) be the head of Christ? For the purpose of salvation the Son has subordinated himself to the Father, and the Spirit has subordinated himself to the Son and to the Father. It is a voluntary subordination in order that salvation may be carried out. It is essential in the carrying out of the work. The Son said, 'Here am I, send me'. He volunteered. He lays aside this aspect of equality, he becomes a servant of his Father, and the Father sends him—'the head of Christ is God'. That is the way in which the apostle puts it: 'As the head of Christ is God, so Christ is the head of the man, and so the man is the head of the woman;' therefore 'Wives, submit yourselves unto your own husbands, as unto the Lord'.

That is the positive exposition of this tremendous teaching which alone gives us a true view of marriage. Incidentally, I have been dealing with an argument, a foolish argument again, that is so often brought forward. Somebody says, 'You know, this is quite wrong, I know many instances where the wife is a much abler person than the husband, much more gifted in every respect. Are you saying that such a brilliantly gifted woman has to subject herself to her husband, to a man who is altogether her inferior?' There is only one answer to that argument; the person who frames it is arguing against God. God knows all about such cases. What God says is that if that gifted, brilliant woman is not subjecting herself to her own husband she is sinning. Whatever her gifts she is to submit to her partner in marriage.

At this point I would make two comments. No woman, whatever her gifts, has a right even to contemplate marrying a given individual unless she is prepared to submit in that way. It is a voluntary submission, it is the way in which Christ submitted and subordinated himself. She is to behave in the same way, and unless she is prepared to do so, unless she is convinced that she can submit herself to this man, she should not marry him. If she enters into marriage with any other idea, it is against the will of God, and she is committing sin.

My second comment is this. I sometimes think that one of the most wonderful things I have ever been privileged to witness was a case of this very thing to which I am referring actually being put into practice. It was my custom for a number of years to go and preach in a certain church in the provinces, and after preaching to spend the night in the manse with the minister and his wife. It was always most interesting for this reason, that it was so obvious to me on the first visit, that from the standpoint of sheer ability there was no comparison between the husband and the wife. The wife was an exceptionally able and brilliant woman. The husband was not without his gifts, but his main gifts were in the matter of personality—he was an exceptionally nice and friendly and kind and gracious man. But as regards sheer intellectual ability there was no comparison. Indeed their academic record—they were both graduates—had proved this. The wife had a degree in a subject that very few women took up at that particular time, and she had taken first class honours. The husband, taking a much easier subject, only had a second class. There was no question, I say, as to the ability—her grasp of intellectual matters, her understanding, struck me immediately, and became more and more evident as I got to know them. But what I wish to say is that I do not know that I have ever seen anything more wonderful than the way in which that woman always put her husband into his true scriptural position. She did it in a very clever and subtle way.

She would put arguments into his mouth; but she always did so in such a way as to suggest that they were his, and not hers! There is an amusing aspect to the matter, but I am reporting it as one of the most moving and tremendous things I have ever experienced. She was not only an able woman, she was a Christian woman, and she was putting into operation this principle that the husband is the head. He always had to state the decision though she had supplied him with the reasons. She was acting as a help meet for him. She had the qualities that he lacked; she was complementing, she was supplementing him. But the husband was the head, and the children were always referred to him. She was guarding his position.

Let me show the importance of realizing and grasping and understanding this teaching. Why is all this so important, and especially today? Why is it more important that I should have been doing what I have been doing rather than giving my opinions on politics or some international problem? It is because the failure to understand and to implement this very teaching is the cause of most of the problems in the world today. The basic problem in the world today is the problem of authority. The chaos in the world is due to the fact that people in every realm of life have lost all respect for authority, whether it be between nations or between parts of nations, whether it be in industry, whether it be in the home, whether it be in the schools, or anywhere else. The loss of authority! And in my view it all really starts in the home and in the married relationship. That is why I venture to query whether a statesman whose own marriage has broken down really has a right to speak about the world's problems. If he fails in the sphere where he is most competent, what right has he to speak in others? He ought to retire out of public life. The real breakdown starts in the home, and in the married relationhip. I am asserting that the appalling increase in divorce which has taken place since the Second World War (I am told it is coming down a little at the moment, but I suggest that that is only temporary and can be explained) is due to one thing only, namely, that men and women do not understand this scriptural teaching about marriage and about husbands and wives.

The same lack of understanding is also the explanation of the breakdown in family and in home life, which is again so obvious at the present time. The family is ceasing to be the centre that it used to be. The members of the family are always out somewhere, and often out at all hours of the night. Family life with its wonderful cohesion—this fundamental unit in life—is disappearing. We find here, too, the explanation of the unruliness and the indiscipline amongst children, and therefore the main explanation of juvenile delinquency. This can be proved even from statistics! Children who have become delinquents are almost invariably the children of broken homes, broken marriages. They have never been given a chance, as we say. They have been brought up in an atmosphere of uncertainty, indecision, and conflict, where wife is against husband and husband against wife, and they become cynics in their tender years. They have no respect for either father or mother, or for anybody or anything. The place where a child should have confidence, and should be able to look for authority and leadership and guidance has gone; there is nothing there, and so the poor child becomes a delinquent. He has been brought up in this atmosphere of conflict between father and mother, husband and wife.

Indeed, there are other aspects of this trend that seem to me to be even more sinister. Is it not a fact that, increasingly, men have been abrogating their position and retiring out of it, and not doing their duty as husbands and as fathers as the result of sheer laziness and selfishness? Husbands are increasingly leaving the discipline of home-life to the wives, to the mothers. They cannot be bothered; they come home tired from work and ask their wives to keep the children from them, and to answer their questions. Is not this happening increasingly? The husband is deliberately vacating the position in which God has put him. It is happening among Christian people, but it is happening still more among non-Christians. The husband is evacuating his position, and leaving it in his laziness to the wife.

This is happening today in many other directions also. So many Christian people today will not touch politics because they say it is a 'dirty game'. But what an appalling argument! It is their duty as citizens of the country to be interested and concerned. But, here, we are particularly concerned with this realm of marriage.

Then, on the other side, feminism has led to aggressiveness on the part of the wife, the mother. She is setting herself up as an equal, and undermining the influence of the father in the minds of the children. The unhappy result is the totally false and wrong approach to the whole question. I do not say this in a spirit of criticism. We are seeing this increasingly in this country, but to nothing like the extent to which they are seeing it in the United States of America. There, you have what may more or less be called a matriarchal society, and the man is becoming increasingly regarded merely as the one to provide the dollars, the wage-earner, the man who brings in the necessary money. The woman, the mother, is the cultured person, and the head of the home; and the children look to her. This false unscriptural view of man and woman, and father and mother leads to a matriarchal society, which, it seems to me, is most dangerous. The result is, of course, the growth of crime and all the terrible social problems with which they are grappling in that country. Then, because they influence every other country through their films and in various other ways, this attitude is being spread throughout the entire world. A matriarchal society with the woman as the head and centre of the home is a denial of the biblical teaching, and is, indeed, a repetition of the old sin of Eve.

The problem is being recognized increasingly. That is why marriage guidance councils and suchlike bodies have been formed. But, alas, they generally approach the problems in terms of psychology. Yet if you examine the married life of many of these psychologists you get a shock. These people who give advice as to how marriages are to be entered into, how they are to be preserved and kept, cannot apply the teaching in their own marriages. Of course, they cannot! It is not a matter of psychology. What is needed is not just a little common sense and wisdom and the spirit of comradeship, and give and take. Men and women know all about that, and have known all about it always; but they cannot practise it. No, there is only one hope. Until God is the authority, and man and wife submit themselves to him, until they do all things 'as unto the Lord', and realize that it is the same sort of headship as that of God over Christ, and Christ over man, there is no hope. It is as men and women in the last hundred years have increasingly departed from the authority of the Bible that this terrible social blight and problem has become more and more evident. I know that I shall be told, 'You obviously want to go back to that stern, repressive, autocratic Victorian husband and father'. That is quite wrong! I know that much of the modern problem is due to a reaction against Victorianism, and I condemn Victorianism as much as the present position. We must come back to the Bible. I am not advocating a return to the Victorian idea. I say, Come back to God, come back to Christ, come back to the revelation in the authoritative Word of God. Look again at his perfect plan—man, and the woman by his side complementing him, his help meet; loving one another, revering, respecting, honouring one another, but never confusing the two spheres.

May God in his grace enable us not only to see the teaching, but to submit ourselves to it, and thereby bring honour and glory to the name of the blessed Lord. 'As unto the Lord'.

3. The Analogy of the Body

Ephesians 5:22-24

W E COME BACK TO THIS STATEMENT, because so far we have been able to look at one aspect only of it in detail. The apostle gives us two great particular reasons why wives should submit themselves to their own husbands. We have considered the first, which is that it is a matter of the order of nature. He says: 'For the husband is the head of the wife', God ordained it so when he made man and woman at the beginning; and we have seen how the New Testament not only confirms that but constantly goes back to that original ordinance of God. So here we are dealing with something that is basic and fundamental to the whole of man's life on earth, and to his wellbeing.

Now in all this, we have not yet been saying anything that is peculiarly and specifically Christian. That was the teaching of the Old Testament, that is something that everybody should recognize, whether they are Christians or not. This is God's ordinance with regard to the whole of life. As we have recognized the family we are to recognize this. The God who ordained the family ordained marriage, the God who ordained the state ordained marriage; and as we should submit ourselves to the state, so we should pay heed to this fundamental ordinance of God with regard to the relative positions of husbands and wives, and the relationship that should subsist between them. Now all that, so far, is general. The fact that we are Christians does not mean that we have no interest in what is general; the fact that we are Christians does not mean that we do not need the Old Testament. It is still there as a foundation; we build upon it; that is why the apostle puts it first.

But now he goes on to his second reason, which is a peculiarly Christian one, 'The husband is the head of the wife'.
Then comes the Christian addition—'even as Christ is the head
of the church'. This takes us further; it does not do away with
the first, but it adds to it, and indeed it helps us to understand
the first. That is what the Christian faith does with regard to
the whole of life. It is only a Christian who can really appreciate life in general in this world. I mean that it is only a Christian, in the last analysis, who can really enjoy nature. The
Christian sees nature in a different way from the man of the
world. There is a newness about it. He does not merely see the
thing in and of itself, he sees the great Creator and the wonder
of his ways, the variety, the colour and the beauty. In other
words, being a Christian means that your whole outlook upon
life is enriched. It does not matter what it is, every gift that
man has, and which he manifests, can only be truly appreciated
by the Christian. He sees with a greater depth, he has a fuller
understanding. That is to say, the Christian message not only
adds to what we had before but it greatly enriches what we
had before, and gives us a deeper insight into it. Here we shall
find that this specifically Christian addition not only helps us
to understand the order of nature already laid down, but that
further, on top of that, it adds a new quality, another aspect as
it were, another emphasis to it all.

Here is the statement: 'The husband is the head of the wife,
even as Christ is the head of the church: and he is the saviour of the body'. What we are looking at here is something
that only a Christian can understand; no-one else can. A man
who does not believe in the Lord Jesus Christ, and who does
not know the way of salvation, obviously cannot understand
what Scripture means in saying that 'Christ is the head of the
body, which is the church. It is meaningless to him; he does
not understand it at all. Such a person therefore cannot understand this specifically Christian view of marriage. This is a

deduction from the Christian doctrine of the church; and therefore if a man does not understand the Christian doctrine of the church, according to the apostle he cannot finally understand the Christian view of marriage.

This leads us at once to draw certain conclusions. The first is, that obviously a Christian should never marry a non-Christian. We are told that specifically in the Second Epistle to the Corinthians: 'Be ye not unequally yoked together with unbelievers' (2 *Cor.* 6:14). That is undoubtedly a reference to this question of marriage. And if we needed a reason for accepting that exhortation we have it here. If believer marries unbeliever the position would be that one of the people getting married would have this exalted Christian view of marriage, while the other would know nothing at all about it. Already there would be a defect in the marriage. They are not one in it; they are not entering into it in the same way; there is already a division; the one has something the other has not got. There is already the seed of discord, as the apostle proves in that same statement in 2 Corinthians chapter 6.

The second deduction I would draw is that a Christian service in connection with marriage is only appropriate for Christians. This is a very large subject, it is a part of the subject of the discipline of the Christian church. The position has become quite chaotic, and people who know nothing at all about Christianity are given a Christian service in which this statement is read out about the husband being the head of the wife 'even as Christ is the head of the church'. It is quite meaningless to them. I deduce therefore that that should not be done. You do not teach high Christian doctrine to those who are not Christians; to them you preach nothing but repentance and the need of belief. They cannot possibly understand the doctrine concerning marriage. You have to be in the Christian life before you can understand it. I am arguing therefore that a Christian service at a wedding should be reserved only and exclusively for Christians. It is to make a farce of it to have such a service for any others.

Thirdly, I deduce that such a service is appropriate and right, and should be taken and conducted, when Christian people are being married. I mean this. Some of the Puritans, 300 years ago, in their violent reaction against Roman Catholicism, decided that there should be no service at all in connection with marriage. Marriage, they said, is nothing but a legal contract. Now we can well understand their reaction and we are in great sympathy with it. The Roman church had taught the false and unbiblical view that marriage is a sacrament so the Puritans felt that they must get as far away as they could from that idea. Hence they ceased to have a service at all. But surely, in the light of the apostle's teaching here, that was quite wrong! It was too violent a reaction, so violent that it became unscriptural. There are aspects of marriage which demand a service—the teaching and the understanding of this particular scripture, and others. And as the teaching is that marriage is something comparable to the mystical union between Christ and his church, I say that it is an occasion for worship and for a truly Christian service. Marriage is not only a legal contract, and we must be very careful, as I have been pointing out, that we do not allow people whose thinking is wrong to govern our thinking and our behaviour. The Christian must never be merely a reaction against anything; he must be positive, he must be scriptural. But there are those who in their hatred of Roman Catholicism go so far to the other side that they end by denying the very Scripture that they claim to uphold.

However, let me go on to assert that, though the Christian view of marriage immediately suggests those three things, it does not here, nor anywhere else, teach, as the Roman Catholics teach, that marriage is a sacrament. There is no teaching whatsoever anywhere in the Bible to support that idea. I defy anyone to produce such a scripture. Marriage is not a sacrament. What then is the teaching? It is that which is given here, namely, this whole idea of the mystical union. The relationship between husband and wife, and wife and husband, is comparable to that between Christ and the church and the church and Christ. The apostle for our comfort says later on, 'This is a great mystery'! The relationship between Christ and the church is a mystery. It is a fact, but it is a great mystery — this mystical union between the church and Christ and the individual believer and Christ. But being fact, we must increasingly try to understand it. Paul says that the relationship between husband and wife, and wife and husband, is comparable to that fact. It belongs to that order, and that is the way in which we must begin to think of it. We are introduced here to the realm of this high doctrine concerning the Christian church.

The apostle, with his logical mind, knows that there should be no difficulty about this in the minds of these Ephesians, because he has already taught them about that very doctrine. He did so in chapter 1 where he prays at the end that they might know 'what is the exceeding greatness of God's power toward them'. He says it is the power 'manifested in Christ when he raised him from the dead . . . And hath put all things under his feet, and gave him to be the head over all things to the church, which is his body, the fulness of him that filleth all in all'. There, Paul has introduced them to the doctrine of the church; here he is applying it. People who rush to the end of an epistle without reading the beginning are always in error. What we have here are deductions. He did the same thing again and added a little more to the definition, in chapter 4 in verses 15 and 16 where he says:

> Speaking the truth in love, may grow up into him in all things, which is the head, even Christ: from whom the whole body fitly joined together and compacted by that which every joint supplieth, according to the effectual working in the measure of every part, maketh increase of the body unto the edifying of itself in love.

He now draws upon that teaching in order that they may understand the true nature of Christian marriage.

What is the point? It is essentially this. He is emphasizing the organic, the vital union, the intimate relationship. He has referred to 'bands of supply' in chapter 4 verse 16, those 'sheaths', as it were, the nerves and the arteries, which bring sustenance from the head, from the centre, to every part of the body. That is a way of stressing this vital organic union that exists between a husband and a wife. It is one life, and it is one life in the same way as the life of the church in her relationship to the head, which is Christ. Here, of course, the apostle is particularly interested in one aspect of all that, the aspect of dependence: 'Wives, submit yourselves unto your own husbands, as unto the Lord. For the husband is the head of the wife, even as Christ is the head of the church'. He is dealing with this aspect of dependence and of submission, and he introduces this further element in order that we may have a clear understanding of how it comes in, and why it comes in inevitably. Later on he will deal with the other side of it, the husband with respect to the wife.

As we consider this great statement we are confronted at once by a problem. Look at it again: 'For the husband is the head of the wife, even as Christ is the head of the church—and he is the saviour of the body'. The problem that engages so much of the attention of the commentators, and rightly so, is this. Why did the apostle add this further statement? Why did he not say, 'The husband is the head of the wife, even as Christ is the head of the church... Therefore as the church is subject unto Christ, so let the wives be to their own husbands in everything'? Why did he add, 'and he is the saviour of the body'? There are those—and they are in the majority, and they include great names, for example, Charles Hodge—who do not hesitate to say at this point that this is a purely independent addition, and that what the apostle is referring to when

he says 'he is the saviour of the body' is clearly that the Lord
Jesus Christ is the saviour of the church. They go on to say
that this has nothing to do with the husband. Why then did
Paul say it? Well, they say, he said it for this reason. He had
committed himself to this, that the husband is the head of the
wife, even as Christ is the head of the church, and the very
mention of the name of Christ makes him cry out 'and he is
the saviour of the body'. It has nothing to do with what he is
arguing at the moment, but the very mention of the name of
Christ makes him say this wonderful thing. So, they argue that
this is an independent phrase, and that it does not apply to the
husband's relationship to the wife.

Their arguments are these: They ask, Can you say that the
husband is the saviour of his wife as Christ is the saviour of the
church? That, they say, is nonsense. Christ, we know, died for
the church. He saves us by his atoning death and by his resurrection; but you cannot say that about any other relationship.
It is quite unique. The apostle was just carried away by the
depth of his feeling, and put in this independent phrase which
obviously has nothing to do with the husband/wife relationship.

What do we say with respect to that? We have to grant, of
course, that if you read a statement like this superficially and
without examining it carefully, you would have to agree with
it. There is no need to argue about this. Christ as saviour of the
church, in that sense, is unique, and that obviously does not
apply to the husband.

But that is not the whole of their argument. They have a further argument to which they attach very great importance. It
is based upon the word translated 'Therefore' at the beginning
of verse 24. The verse runs thus: '*Therefore* as the church is
subject unto Christ, so let the wives be to their own husbands
in everything'. The point they make here is this. They say that
the translation 'Therefore' is quite wrong; and, indeed, they are

right in saying that. But then they go on to say that the word which is translated 'Therefore' should in reality be translated 'Nevertheless'. It is a word of contrast, and it always presents a contrast. So they say that we should read it like this: 'For the husband is the head of the wife, even as Christ is the head of the church and he is the saviour of the body. Nevertheless'— though that is not true of the husband with respect to the wife, in spite of that—'Nevertheless let the wives be subject to their own husbands in everything'. So they feel that the case is quite unanswerable; that the apostle himself says in effect, 'Now when I said that he is the saviour of the body I had forgotten for the moment my analogy between the relationship of Christ and the church, and the husband and the wife—"Nevertheless"—in spite of that, though that is not true in the realm of husband and wife, the wives should still submit themselves to their own husbands even as the church is subject unto Christ.'

It seems to me that there is an adequate answer to all this argumentation. First of all, it confines the meaning of the word 'saviour'. The word 'saviour' does not always carry that one meaning, of Christ giving his life for the church, and his blood being shed. It is the common meaning, but it is not the only meaning; there is a wider meaning to this term 'saviour'. There is an example of this in the First Epistle to Timothy, chapter 4 and verse 10: 'For therefore', says the apostle, 'we both labour and suffer reproach, because we trust in the living God, who is the saviour of all men, specially of those that believe'. Now that is exactly the same word as is used here about 'the saviour of the body'. There we are told that God, the living God, is the saviour of all men, especially of those that believe. You cannot say that that means that all men enjoy salvation in a spiritual sense, because that would make you universalists. Of course not! Well then, it means that the word 'saviour' there has a different connotation. What it means there is 'preserver'—that he looks after, that he cares for. He is the preserver of all men, especially of those that believe. We are reminded by our Lord, 'He causes his sun to rise upon the evil and the good, and he sends rain upon the just and upon the unjust'; yes, and gives food to all. It is in that sense he is the saviour of all men. So why not give that meaning to the word 'saviour' here? He is the one who looks after and safeguards the body. That is one reply which we can put up against the argument quoted.

But I have further reasons for rejecting that exposition which would confine this little phrase solely to the Lord Jesus Christ and his saving work. My second reason is this: I would argue that verses 28 and 29, which are to follow, insist upon our interpreting this phrase as applying to the husband and wife as well as to Christ and the church: Paul says, 'So ought men to love their wives as their own bodies. He that loveth his wife loveth himself. For no man ever yet hated his own flesh.' Well, what does he do ? 'He nourisheth and cherisheth it'—yes, he is acting as a saviour to it, he is looking after it, he is preserving it. 'No man ever yet hated his own flesh; but nourisheth and cherisheth it, even as the Lord the church, which is His body'—and so on. He says the husband ought to deal with his wife as his own flesh, his own body. He does not neglect his own body, he nourishes it and cherishes it. In other words he is 'the saviour of the body'. How important it is always to take a verse in its context! Even the mighty can fall at this point. I argue that those two verses insist upon this other interpretation here, and that this is not an isolated independent phrase, true only of the Lord Jesus Christ. Paul is still talking about husbands and wives, 'The husband is the head of the wife, even as Christ is the head of the church: and he is the saviour of the body'. It is true of both.

But what of the word which is translated 'therefore' at the beginning of verse 24? Now this is really interesting. I have gone to the trouble of consulting some of the best lexicons on the point. It is a Greek word, *Alla*, and I find that it need not be translated always as a kind of antithesis to something which is an opposite and a contrast. Take, for instance, the Greek/English Lexicon of the New Testament (edition 1952), by Arndt and Gingrich, one of the best and most authoritative. They actually say this: that what it really means is 'now' or 'then'. I quote them. They say, 'It is used to strengthen the command', not to imply a contrast or a difference, to strengthen the very command that he is giving. And they actually pick out Ephesians 5:24 as an illustration of this particular use of the word. Grimm-Thayer has a similar statement.

It seems to me therefore that on all these grounds we must reject the interpretation which says that this is an independent phrase referring only to the Lord. Indeed, if it were that, it would be quite purposeless at this point; it would be sheer confusion. This apostle is not given to doing that kind of thing. So what we read, therefore, is that 'the husband is the head of the wife, even as Christ is the head of the church; and he is the saviour of the body'. Then—'As the church is subject unto Christ, so let the wives be to their husbands in everything'.

What, then, is the doctrine? It is clearly this. The wife is the one who is kept, preserved, guarded, shielded, provided for by the husband. That is the relationship—as Christ nourishes and cherishes the church, so the husband nourishes and cherishes the wife—and the wife should realize that that is her position in this relationship. The husband is the preserver, he is the saviour of the body. The wife then should start with this idea, and she should always act in the light of it.

But we can go further. What is the relationship of the body to the head? What is true of the church in relation to Christ is true of the wife in relation to the husband. Let us take the illustration that Paul uses here and in the previous instances I have given of the church as the body of Christ such as in 1 Corinthians chapter 12 and Romans chapter 12. What is the teaching? The wife is to the husband what the body is to the head, what the church is to Christ. It is the idea of the 'complement' again. The essential thing in the Christian concept of marriage is this idea of wholeness, completeness. We met with it in Genesis chapter 2—'help meet', someone taken out of Adam, a part of him; yes, but complementing him, making up a wholeness. That is the very idea that you think of inevitably as you think of your body, the body as a whole. The body is not a collection of parts, not a number of fingers and hands and feet and toes stuck on, and limbs loosely attached together. That is a completely false notion of the body. It is an organic, vital unity; it is one, it is whole. Now that is the very idea we have here. The husband and wife are not separate; they are not like two kingdoms which have diplomatic relationships, but are always in a state of tension, and always in danger of a quarrel. That is quite the opposite of the Christian concept of what a marriage really is. Christ and the church are one as the body and the head are one. But this ideal allows for differing functions; and that is what we are to grasp—differing functions, different purposes, special duties that only each part can perform. But it is vital that we should remember that each part is a part of a whole and that all the separate actions are part of a unified action which leads to a corporate result.

But let us work this out a little more in detail in order to illumine this question of the marriage state and relationship. How important all this is! I have given some reasons for that already. I believe that much of the irreligion of today is partly a reaction against that Victorian type of life in which many husbands and wives appeared to be great Christians, but of whom people said, 'If only you knew them in their private life!' Nothing does more harm to Christianity than that a man should not be the same at home as he is in the church or out on the street or in his office. It is in the home you really know a man. What are the relationships there? These things are important for that reason, not only in and of themselves, but as a part of our general testimony as Christians.

What, then, does this teach us about the relationship of the wife to the husband in this matter of subjecting herself? It seems clear that it does not teach a mere and a sheer passivity; the wife is not to be entirely passive. It is a mis-interpretation of this picture to say that the wife should never speak, never give an opinion, but be mute or dumb and utterly passive. That is a pressing of an analogy and an illustration to a point at which it becomes meaningless. But what it means is this: the wife should never be guilty of independent action. The analogy of the body and the head insists upon that. The business of my body is not to act independently of me. It is I who decide to act with my mind and brains and will. My body is the means through which I express it. If my body begins to act apart from me, I am suffering from some sort of 'convulsions'. This is exactly what 'convulsions' means; that parts of a man's body are moving in an irrational manner. It is not purposive action; he does not want them to act, but he cannot stop them; they are acting independently of his mind and will. That is chaos, that is convulsions. Here is the analogy, 'Wives, submit yourselves unto your own husbands; be subject and obedient to them in everything'. Why? Because as wife, and in this relationship, you do not act independently of your husband. If you do, it is chaos, it is convulsions.

Or let me divide it up still more. The wife must not act before the husband. All the teaching indicates that he is the head, that he ultimately controls. So she not only does not act independently of him, she does not act before him. But let me emphasize this also; as it is true to say that she must not act before him, it is equally true to say that she must not delay action, she must not stall action, she must not refuse to act. Go back to the analogy of the body. Think of somebody who has had a stroke. This person wants to act, but the limb is paralysed, so he cannot. Though the person is willing movement there is no movement—the arm is not healthy, it resists movement. This is a part of the teaching; the subjection involves the idea that she does not act before her husband, nor does she delay, she does not hinder action, she does not paralyse action. These points are all vital in this whole relationship of marriage; and it is because people do not realize and know these things that marriage is breaking down round and about us. Independence, acting before, not acting, stalling, refusing, is all wrong; and it is all because men and women do not understand this Christian view of marriage.

We can sum it up thus: The teaching is that the initiative and the leadership are ultimately the husband's, but the action must always be co-ordinated. That is the meaning of this picture—co-ordinated action but leadership in the head. There is no sense of inferiority suggested by this. The wife is not inferior to her husband; she is different. She has her own peculiar position, full of honour and respect. That is why the man is later to be told to cherish and to nourish and to love and to care for, and to respect and honour his wife. There is no inferiority involved. What Paul is teaching is that any Christian woman who realizes all this will love to please her husband, to be useful to him, to help him, to aid him, to enable him to function. She will not cavil at saying 'and obey' in the marriage service. What a sad thing this is! I was told by a friend recently that a clergyman who was going to take a marriage service had said that he would not have the word 'obey'. He thought he was being modern, that he was appealing to 'the man in the street'—showing that, after all, Christianity is not narrow! He did not realize that he was denying the biblical doctrine. And how utterly inconsistent such people are! Such a man, I suppose, if he was in a football match, would boast of the fact of the team spirit. Though they are all playing individually and all have ability, they start off by saying that there is only one man who is captain. Each says 'I am not captain, I am submitting myself to the captain'. That is marvellous, that is the team spirit; each player is going to obey the captain. But you must not say that with regard to marriage! That is derogatory to woman, that is old-fashioned, that is Paul, that is the hard pharisee, that is legalistic, that is the Old Testament! But that denies the whole doctrine, and is even inconsistent in its supposed modernity. The Christian wife, understanding these things, wants to say 'and obey', 'to love, cherish and obey'. Of course! Why is she getting married? Is it not in order to produce 'one flesh', wholeness? Is it not in order to enjoy this co-ordinated action, this completeness, which is to be demonstrated to the world? That is not slavery; that is living as the church does with respect to her Lord; that is manifesting the essential spirit of Christianity.

But let me say a final word. Did you notice that the end of the exhortation was, 'Therefore (then, now then) as the church is subject unto Christ, so let the wives be to their own husbands in everything'. 'Everything!' Does it really mean that? Here we answer again in terms of the analogy of Scripture in its entirety. When the Scripture makes a sweeping general statement like that it always expects us to interpret it in the light of its own teaching. So when we read here that the wife is to be subject to her own husband in everything, it is exactly the same as saying that the Christian is to be subject to the state, to the powers that be, as in Romans chapter 13 and in other places. Does it mean, then, that the wife has to do literally everything her husband tells her to do in all circumstances and conditions? Of course not! That would be to make the Scripture ridiculous. There are qualifications here. What are they? Here is one: It is a fundamental rule of the Scripture that nobody should ever act against his or her conscience. This exhortation does not tell a wife that she has to act against her own conscience. Within the conjugal relation, within the terms of marriage, the husband has no right to dictate to a wife's conscience.

Here we might cite a number of very interesting cases. There is a great deal of confusion sometimes between obeying conscience and holding on to an opinion. They are not the same thing. The Scripture exhorts us to obey conscience in all circumstances; but that is not necessarily the same thing as holding on to your own opinion. Let me give you one illustration of this. I remember reading in the book on Scottish theology by Dr John Macleod, of a very interesting case that teaches this very point. There was a dispute in Scotland in the eighteenth century over the relationship of the Christian to the local government, and part of the church divided into two sections known as the Burgher and the anti-Burgher sections. This was a matter of great controversy. There was a minister of the name of James Scott who had a very remarkable wife whose name was Alison. She was the daughter of that very remarkable man Ebenezer Erskine, one of the founders of the original Secession in Scotland. She was a very strong character and also the wife of a very able man. Mr Scott and his wife disagreed at this point—Mr Scott belonging to the anti-Burgher party, Mrs Scott belonging to the Burgher party. Many difficult cases arose, and Mr Scott was in a synod which actually reprimanded and deposed his wife's father and uncle and brother-in-law—a very courageous act on his part. Then, having done that in the synod he had to go home and tell his wife what he had done. In response, Alison Scott made this famous statement: 'James Scott, you are still my husband but you are no longer my minister'. She also put that into practice, so that as every Sunday came she did not go and worship in the church where her own husband was leading the service and preaching, she went to one of the Burgher churches. What do you make of a case like that? I would not hesitate to say that Alison Scott was entirely wrong, because she was putting opinion in the place of conscience. There, surely, is an instance where, for every reason, she should have submitted to the leading and the guidance of her husband. She would not have been violating her conscience; it was a pure matter of opinion. We must never, I say, make the mistake of confusing conscience and opinion. The wife can give her opinion, but when she sees that the husband is determined, she should abide by his ruling.

Let me give you another illustration to counter-balance this one. One of the most remarkable and moving experiences I have ever had since I have been the minister of Westminster Chapel happened some eighteen months ago, if I remember rightly. I was preaching in the chapel on the first Sunday night after I had come back from my summer vacation, and on the text 'We are ambassadors for Christ'. I was emphasizing the aspect of the call of the ambassador, and so on. I went out of the pulpit into my room, and a lady was ushered in immediately, obviously in a state of agitation. What she had to tell me was this, that she was quite certain that that sermon had been preached for her. She and her husband had been married for some ten years. He had the feeling that he was being called to the ministry, and he was giving up his work as a school teacher. She did not agree at all. She had done everything she could to hinder her husband, but still the husband was certain and was going forward, and there was a real crisis in their married life. But during the service that woman had been deeply convicted about this matter, and just came in to confess it to me and to tell me that she was rushing immediately to the nearest telephone to phone her husband who was down in the West Country, and who had to sit an examination for entrance into the ministry the very next morning. She saw how wrong she had been to stand on her opinion and thus to thwart God's purpose in her husband's life. That was not conscience, that was standing on an opinion. I say that we should never violate conscience, but I also say that we must be ready to submit in the matter of opinion. The wife's position in the married relationship is not to be pressed to the extent of going against her conscience; neither must she allow her husband to make her commit sin. If the husband is trying to get the wife to commit sin she must say 'No!' Not to say this is to make the Scripture ridiculous. Should the husband lose his mental balance and become insane, obviously she is not to obey him in everything. The Scripture is never ridiculous; the Scripture carries its own meaning with it; and there are these inevitable limits.

The fourth point I would make is that the wife is not to submit to the husband to the extent of allowing him to interfere with her relationship to God and the Lord Jesus Christ. She must do everything short of that, but not that!

Fifthly, adultery breaks the marriage relationship; and if the husband has been guilty of adultery the wife is no longer bound to give him obedience in everything. She can divorce him, she is allowed to do so by the Scripture. She is entitled to do so because adultery breaks the unity, breaks the relationship. They are now separate and no longer one. He has broken the unity, he has gone out of it. So we must not interpret this Scripture as teaching that the wife is thus irrevocably, inevitably bound to an adulterous husband for the rest of her life. She may choose to be—that is for her to decide. All I am saying is, that this Scripture does not command it, it does not make it inevitable. In other words, there are these limits to these matters.

There, then, as I see it, are the main deductions from this wonderful illustration. The big point that is emphasized is that the wife must go to the extremest limit of submitting herself to her husband for Christ's sake, for the reasons given, short of violating the principles which we have just been laying down. To any wife who is in trouble in this matter let me suggest certain practical helps. If you are in trouble, ask yourself the following questions: Why did I originally marry this man? What was it then? Cannot that be restored? Try to re-capture that in the spirit of Christ and the gospel. 'Ah but,' you say, 'it is impossible, I cannot'. Well then, I say, as a Christian, feel sorry for the man, pray for him. Put into practice the teaching of the Apostle Peter, in his First Epistle, chapter 3, where he tells the wives so plainly to subject themselves, and not only to those who are Christians:

> Be in subjection to your own husbands; that if any obey not the word, they also may without the word be won by the conversation of the wives; while they behold your chaste conversation coupled with fear.

Try to put that into practice; try in humility and meekness to win your husband.

> Whose adorning let it not be that outward adorning of plaiting the hair, and of wearing of gold, or of putting on of apparel; but let it be the hidden man of the heart, in that which is not corruptible, even the ornament of a meek and quiet spirit, which is in the sight of God of great price.

Do all you can, go to the limit, go beyond the limit short of these principles. And, finally, ask yourself this question—Can I honestly go in my present attitude and condition into the presence of the Lord, who, in spite of me and my vileness and my sinfulness, came from heaven and went to the cross of Calvary and gave himself and his life for me? If you can face him all is well; I have nothing to say. But if you feel condemned, in his presence, about your attitude, about your relationship in any aspect, go and put it right. So that when you go back to him again, it will be with a quiet conscience, an open spirit, and you will be able to rejoice in his holy presence. This is a Christian matter; it is like the relationship of the church to Christ, the body to the head. As long as we look at it in those terms there are no problems; it is a great privilege, it is something which God looks down upon with pleasure and with delight. 'Wives, submit yourselves'—'a meek and a quiet spirit is in the sight of God of great price', and however much you may have to suffer here, your reward in heaven will be very great.

4. True Love

Ephesians 5:25-33

SO FAR WE HAVE BEEN LOOKING at what the apostle has to say to wives; now we come to what he has to say to husbands. It is found in the remarkable statement he makes from verse 25 to the end of the chapter. It is remarkable in two main respects; in what it tells us about the duties of husbands, and, still more remarkable, in what it tells us about the relationship of the Lord Jesus Christ to the Christian church. That is one of the astounding things about this man's letters always; you never know when you are going to find a pearl, a pearl of greatest price. Here, in this essentially practical part of this epistle, he suddenly throws out the most exalted and wonderful statement he has ever made anywhere about the nature of the Christian church and her relationship to the Lord Jesus Christ. You observe that in treating this matter of husbands, and how they are to behave towards their wives, he also treats that other subject, and he gives both this wonderful treatment.

The two things, you will notice, are intertwined; so our first business is to arrive at some kind of a division of the matter. He moves from one to the other and then back to the first. That is often his method; he does not always make a complete statement on the one side and then apply it; he gives a part of his statement, applies it, and then another part, and applies that. I suggest this classification. In verses 25, 26 and 27 he tells us what Christ has done for the church, and why he has done it. Then in verses 28 and 29 he gives us a preliminary deduction from that as to the duty of a husband towards his wife,

55

especially in terms of the union that subsists between Christ and the church, and the husband and the wife. Then in part of verse 29 and in verses 30 and 32 he develops sublime doctrine of the mystical union between Christ and the church. Then in verses 31 and 33 he draws his final practical deductions.

That seems to me to be the analysis of the verses we are studying. But in order that we may grasp his teaching more clearly, I suggest that we approach it in this way. First, we start with his general injunction: 'Husbands, love your wives'. That is what he desires to emphasize above everything. In other words the controlling idea with regard to the husband is to be love. You remember that the controlling idea with respect to the wives was submission — 'Wives, submit yourselves'. Submission on the part of the wife, love on the part of the husband! We must be clear about this. This does not mean, of course, that it is the husband alone that is to love. 'He does not say a word here about the wives loving their husbands', someone may remark. To say that is to misunderstand the apostle's object altogether. He is not giving us an exhaustive treatise here on marriage. In his idea of the wife submitting herself love is implicit. We must realize what the apostle is concerned to do. He is really concerned about one basic point only, namely, harmony and peace and unity as they are displayed in the married relationship and in the home. That being his leading theme he picks out on the two sides the element that needs to be emphasized above every other. What the wife is required to keep her eye on, in maintaining the harmony, is the element of submission; while the husband has to keep his eye on the element of love. So Paul is picking out the chief characteristic, the chief contribution that is to be made by each of the partners in this wonderful relationship which can demonstrate the glory of the Christian life so clearly. The word addressed therefore to husbands is, 'Love your wives'.

This is most important, particularly in connection with the previous teaching. It safeguards the previous teaching, and it is important that we should look at it in that way. He has been emphasizing that the husband is 'the head of the wife, even as Christ is the head of the church'. We have seen that he is in the position of leadership, that he is the lord of the wife. That is the teaching of the Old Testament and the New, and the apostle has been emphasizing it. But immediately he adds this: 'Husbands, love your wives', as if to say, 'You are the head, you are the leader, you are as it were the lord in this relationship; but because you love your wives the leadership will never become a tyranny, and though you are "lord" you will never become a tyrant'. That is the connection between the two precepts.

This is something which is found very generally in the teaching of the New Testament. Let me give an example. In many ways the best commentary on this matter is to be found in Paul's Second Epistle to Timothy, chapter 1 and verse 7, where he says, 'God hath not given us the spirit of fear; but of power, and of love, and of a sound mind' (discipline). There you have the same thing again. 'God has not given us the spirit of fear.' Well, what has he given? It is a 'spirit of power'; but lest a man should think that this is something tyrannical he adds, 'and love'. It is the power of love. It is not naked power, it is not the power of a dictator or a little tyrant, it is not the idea of a man who arrogates to himself certain rights, and tramples upon his wife's feelings and so on, and sits in the home as a dictator. I was referring in a previous study to what was perhaps the greatest defect in the Victorian outlook upon life, and even its Christianity; and it was just this very thing. They tended to emphasize one side at the expense of the other. And so many of our problems today are due to a reaction, a violent overreaction against the false emphasis of that particular period.

We must always maintain this balance therefore. We must remember that power is to be tempered by love; it is to be controlled by love, it is the power of love. No husband is entitled to say that he is the head of the wife unless he loves his wife. He is not carrying out the Scriptural injunction unless he does so. These things go together. In other words, it is a manifestation of the Spirit, and the Holy Spirit not only gives power but he gives love and also discipline. So as the husband exercises his privilege as the head of the wife, and the head of the family, he does so in this way. He is to be controlled always by love, and he is to be controlled by discipline. He must discipline himself. There may be the tendency to dictate, but he must not do so—'power, love, sound mind' (discipline). All that is implicit here in this great word 'love'.

So the reign of the husband is to be a reign and a rule of love; it is a leadership of love. It is not the idea of a pope or a dictator; it is not a case of *ipse dixit*; he does not speak *ex-cathedra*. No, it is the power of love, it is the discipline of the Spirit, guarding this power and authority and dignity which are given to the husband. That is clearly the fundamental and the controlling idea in the whole of this matter—'Husbands, love your wives'.

But now we must proceed to consider in general the character or the nature of that love. This again is very much needed at the present time. There are two things which stand out in a glaring manner in the world today—the abuse of the idea of power, and the still greater abuse of the idea of love. The world has never talked so much about love as it does today. But I wonder whether there has ever been a time when there has been less love. These great terms have become so utterly debased that many people have no idea as to the meaning of the word 'love'.

'Husbands, love your wives'. What is this love? Fortunately for us the apostle tells us; and he does so in two ways. 'Husbands, love your wives, even as Christ also loved the church.' There are two definitions there. The first is in the word 'love' itself. The very word the apostle has used here for 'love' is most eloquent in its teaching and its meaning. In the Greek language as used in the days of the Apostle Paul there were three words which can be translated by the English word 'love'. It is most important that we should be clear about this and differentiate between them; because much of the loose thinking today in this realm is due to the failure to appreciate this. One of the three—it does not occur in the New Testament—is the word *eros* which describes a love that belongs entirely to the flesh. The adjective 'erotic', as commonly used today, reminds us of the content of the word. Of course it is a kind of love. But it is a love of the flesh, it is desire, it is something carnal; and the characteristic of that kind of love is that it is selfish. Now it is not of necessity wrong because it is selfish, but that kind of love is essentially selfish; it is born, as I say, of desire. It wants something, and it is mainly concerned about that. That is its level. It is, so to speak, the animal part in man. And that is what generally passes as 'love' in the world today. The world glories in its 'marvellous' romances, and tells us how wonderful they are. Nothing is said, mark you, about the fact that the man has been unfaithful to his wife and vice versa, and that little children are going to suffer. 'A wonderful romance' has come into the life of the man and the woman he is going to marry. That they are both guilty of breaking their vows and desecrating sanctities is not mentioned; what is publicized is this wonderful 'love match', this wonderful romance! You find that kind of thing in the papers every day. It is nothing but this erotic, selfish, fleshly, lustful desire. But I am reminding you that *eros* is certainly regarded as love by the world today.

As for the two words translated 'love' in the New Testament (Authorized Version) one of them, *phileo*, really means 'to be fond of'. It comes in as a root in such words as 'philanthropic' and 'Philadelphia'. The classic illustration of its use is found in the last chapter of the Gospel according to St John in the incident which tells how Peter and the others had gone fishing at night and, coming back, had suddenly seen our Lord on the seashore. There he cooked a breakfast for them, and began to speak to them. This is what we read:

> So when they had dined, Jesus saith to Simon Peter, Simon, son of Jonas, lovest thou me more than these? He saith unto him, Yea, Lord; thou knowest that I love thee. He saith unto him, Feed my lambs.

Now the interesting point there is that when Peter says, 'Thou knowest that I love thee', the word he used was 'Thou knowest that I am fond of thee'. Our Lord, using the third word to which we have not yet come, asks him if he really loves him, but Peter replies, 'Thou knowest that I am fond of thee'. 'He saith unto him again the second time, Simon, son of Jonas, lovest thou me? He saith unto him, Yea, Lord, thou knowest that I love thee' which means, 'Thou knowest that I am fond of thee'—'He saith unto him, Feed my sheep'. Then we come to verse 17: 'He saith unto him the third time, Simon, son of Jonas, lovest thou me?' Now here our Lord does a very interesting thing, he does not use the word he had been using before; he now uses the word that Peter had been using. 'He saith unto him the third time, Simon, son of Jonas, are you really fond of me?' He has lowered the conception, 'Art thou really fond of me?' 'Peter was grieved because he said unto him the third time, Lovest thou me? And he said unto him, Lord, thou knowest all things, thou knowest that I love thee'. Peter was grieved that the Lord seemed to doubt whether he was even fond of him, so in the light of his failure he could but trust himself to the Lord's knowledge and say, 'Thou knowest that I am fond of thee'. But let us keep these things in mind—the word translated as 'love' may mean 'being fond of'.

The other New Testament word rises to a much greater height. This is the word that is always used in the Bible to express God's love to us. 'God so loved the world'—*Agapao*. Now this is the word which is used in the text we are considering.

'Husbands, love your wives' in that sense, love as God loves. There is nothing higher than this. Or, to put it in another way, take the list describing the fruit of the Spirit in Galatians 5:22. The apostle is contrasting the works of the flesh and the fruit of the Spirit, and he says, 'The fruit of the Spirit is love'— not erotic feeling, not merely being fond of, it is the love that resembles God's love—love, joy, peace, and so on. That is the love, says the apostle, which husbands should have and show towards their wives. You see how it all links up so perfectly with the eighteenth verse: 'Be not drunk with wine, wherein is excess, but be filled with the Spirit'. If you are filled with the Spirit you will be filled with the fruit of the Spirit, and the fruit of the Spirit is 'love'.

The apostle is addressing people who are filled with the Spirit, for they alone can show this love. It is idle to say this to a man who is not a Christian. He is incapable of it; he cannot love with this kind of love. But the apostle says that Christians should manifest this kind of love because they are filled with the Spirit. So one of the ways in which I show that I am filled with the Spirit is not so much that I go into ecstasies and manifest certain phenomena; it is the way I behave towards my wife when I am at home, it is this love which is 'the fruit of the Spirit'.

The very word the apostle selects leads us immediately to the precise idea he is anxious to convey. Let me put it in these terms therefore. Let us get this whole question of marriage and the marriage relationship into focus. I am not saying that the apostle teaches that that first element which belongs to the flesh should not come in at all. That is quite wrong. There have been people who have so taught. The Roman Catholic teaching concerning celibacy is ultimately based on that misconception. And there are many Christians, I find, who are in trouble over the matter. They seem to think that the Christian is no longer human, no longer natural; and they regard sex as evil. Now that is not only not Christian teaching, it is error, it is wrong. That element of *eros* is to come in, it is included. Man is man. God made him thus. God has given us these gifts, sex included. There is nothing wrong in the erotic element in and of itself; indeed I go further, I say that it should be present. I refer to this because I am so often asked to deal with these things. I have known Christian people who very honestly, because of this wrong view of sex, and of that which is natural, have more or less come to the conclusion that any Christian man can marry any Christian woman. They say that the only thing that matters and counts now is that we are Christians. They do away altogether with the natural element. But the Bible does not do so. Though we are Christians it is right that we should feel more attracted to one than to another. The natural comes in and you must not exclude it. We must never take up the position that any one of us could quite rightly marry any other. You could live together, but that would be to exclude this natural element.

I have been at pains to show that the Christian teaching never does away with the natural, with the way in which God has created us. And God has so created us that one feels an attraction to one person more than to another person; and it is mutual. That is right; do not set it aside. It is being assumed here. The apostle is assuming that this man and this woman, because they were attracted to each other, because, if you like, to use the common phrase, they 'fell in love', are married. Christians should behave in that way like everybody else. This is not something mechanical. A Christian does not say, 'Now that I am a Christian I am going to look round and decide whom to marry' in cold blood, as it were. That is not biblical teaching. This may sound eccentric and amusing to some, but there are many Christians who have acted on that very principle. I am speaking out of pastoral experience. They are very honest people, but regarding sex as evil, they get into this false position. But we are not to exclude the natural. The apostle is assuming that this man and this woman have felt this mutual attraction, and that they have been drawn together on that basis.

More than that, the apostle is assuming that they are fond of each other. What I mean by that is that they like the companionship of each other. Let me emphasize that that also is to come into Christian marriage. There are certain natural affinities, and we ignore them at our peril. Again, I have often seen this. Two people have imagined that because they are Christians nothing else matters, and they get married on that basis. But it is very important in the married state that the two persons should be fond of each other. If they are not fond of each other, and have married on the basis of the physical only, it will soon go. That has no permanence in it; but on the other hand, one of the things that has permanence is that the two are fond of each other. There are certain imponderables in this married state. It is good that people who are married should have the same affinities, the same interests, should be attracted by the same things. No matter how much they love each other, if there are fundamental differences in this respect, it will lead to trouble. The problem of married life and living in harmony will be very much greater. It is important, I say, that this second element, the word that Peter kept on using, 'I am fond of thee', should play its part.

The apostle is assuming both considerations. It is probable that some of the Christians had married while they were pagans, and that the marriage included both *eros* and *phileo*. Very well, says Paul, this is where Christianity comes in. Now, because you are Christians, the further element comes in; and it lifts up the other two, it sanctifies them, it gives a glory to them, it gives a splendour to them. That is the difference that Christ makes to marriage. It is only the Christian who is able to rise to this level. There can be happy and successful marriages without this; they do happen still, thank God. There are happy marriages on the natural human level, and they are based on the first two words which I have been using. If you get the first element, plus this fondness for each other, and a certain temperament, they can produce very happy and successful marriages. But it will never rise to this higher level. Yet this is the point to which the apostle wants us to rise. Over and above what is possible to the natural man, there comes in this true love, this love that is of God, the love that he defines in 1 Corinthians 13.

It is clear that the apostle in choosing his word has told us a great deal. It is therefore the duty of every husband who hears or reads this exhortation to examine himself in the light of this word. Are the three elements present in you? Is everything crowned and glorified by this 'love' that can be attributed even to God himself?

But lest we be in any trouble about this, the apostle proceeds to give us a further illustration in the second point he makes. He says, 'Husbands, love your wives, even as' — 'even as Christ also loved the church'. Here again, he shows how anxious he is to help us. The very mention of the name of Christ leads him at once to elaborate the statement. He cannot barely say, 'even as Christ loved the church', he must go further and say

> . . . and gave himself for it; that he might sanctify and cleanse it with the washing of water by the word, that he might present it to himself a glorious church, not having spot, or wrinkle, or any such thing; but that it should be holy and without blemish.

He says all that to help the husband to love his wife as he ought to love his wife.

Why, then, does he elaborate the matter in this way? I believe that there are three main reasons. First, he wants everyone of us to know Christ's great love to us. He wants us to realize the truth about Christ and ourselves and our relationship to him. Why is he so concerned about this? His argument is clearly this—it is only as we realize the truth about the relationship of Christ to the church that we can really function as Christian husbands ought to function. That this might be clear he ends by saying, 'This is a great mystery: but I speak concerning Christ and the church'. But why is he speaking concerning Christ and the church? Why has he led us into that mystery? In order that husbands might know how to love their wives. And that is where the glib and superficial people who jeer at doctrine show their folly and their ignorance. 'Ah', they say, 'those people are only interested in doctrine; we are practical people'. But you cannot be practical without doctrine, you cannot love your wife truly unless you understand something about this doctrine, about this great mystery. 'Ah', say others, 'it is too difficult, I cannot follow it at all'. But if you want to live as a Christian you have got to follow it, you have got to apply your mind, you have got to think, you have got to study, you have got to try to understand, you have got to grapple with it. It is here for you, and if you turn your back on this you are rejecting something God gives you, and you are a terrible sinner. To reject doctrine is a terrible sin. You must never put practice against doctrine because you cannot practise without it. So the apostle takes the trouble to elaborate this wonderful doctrine about the relationship of Christ and the church, not simply for the sake of stating it, important as it is, but in order that you and I at home may love our wives as we ought to love them—'even as Christ loved the church.'

So we can now look at the problem in the following way. The principle which is to control our practice is that the relationship between husband and wife is the same in essence, and in nature, as the relationship between Christ and the church. How do we approach it therefore? We must start by studying the relationship between Christ and the church, and then, and then only, can we look at the relationship between the husband

and the wife. That is what the apostle is doing. 'Husbands, love your wives, even as Christ loved the church'. This said, he tells us exactly how Christ has loved the church. Then, he says, Go and do the same; that is your rule. That is the first great doctrine.

We start then by considering the relationship of Christ and the church. Here is something that concerns all, not husbands only, but all people. What we are told about the relationship of Christ to the church is true of every single one of us. Christ is the husband of the church, Christ is the husband of every single believer. You ask, Where do you find this teaching? I find it, for instance, in the Epistle to the Romans, chapter 7 verse 4: 'Wherefore, my brethren, you also are become dead to the law by the body of Christ; that you should be married to another, even to him who is raised from the dead, that we should bring forth fruit unto God'. Christ is the husband of the church, the church is the bride of Christ. Everyone of us can in that sense look upon the Lord Jesus Christ as our husband, and collectively we do so as members of the Christian church.

What does the apostle tell us about this? The first thing he tells us is about the attitude of the Lord Jesus Christ to the church, of how he looks upon her. Here is instruction for husbands. What is your attitude? How do you look upon your wife? Just here the apostle tells us some marvellous things. Christian people, have you realized that these things are true about you as members of the Christian church? Look at the characteristics of our Lord's attitude towards his bride, the church. He loves her: 'even as Christ loved the church'. What an eloquent expression! He loved her in spite of her unworthiness, he loved her in spite of her deficiencies. Notice what he has to do for her. She needs to be washed, she needs to be cleansed. He saw her in her rags, in her wildness; but he loved her. That is the height of the doctrine of salvation. He loved us, not because of anything in us; he loved us in spite of what was in us, while we were yet sinners'. He loved the ungodly, 'while we were yet enemies'. In all our unworthiness and vileness he loved us. He loved the church, not because she was glorious and beautiful—no, but that he might make her such. Take note of the doctrine, and see what it has to say to husbands. A husband comes up against deficiencies, difficulties, things he feels he can criticize in his wife, but he is to love her 'as Christ loved the church'. That is the kind of love he must show. So much for the first principle.

The second principle is this: 'He gave himself for her'. He was not only ready to sacrifice himself for her. He actually did sacrifice himself for her. Such is Christ's love for the church! He could only save her by giving his life for her; and he gave his life. That is the characteristic of his love.

Then take notice of his great concern for her, and for her wellbeing. He is looking at her. He is concerned about her. He sees the possibilities in her, as it were. He desires her to be perfect. That is why Paul goes on to say, 'That he might sanctify her and cleanse her with the washing of water by the word, that he might present her to himself a glorious church, not having spot, or wrinkle, or any such thing'. You see his interest in her, his love for her, his pride in her. Those are the characteristics of Christ's love to the church—this great desire that she should be perfect. And he is not going to be satisfied until she is perfect. He wants to be able to present her to himself a glorious church, 'not having spot, or wrinkle, or any such thing'. He wants her to be perfect, beyond criticism. He wants the whole world, as it were, to admire her. So we were told in the third chapter of this epistle, in verse 10, that he has done all this 'to the intent that now unto the principalities and powers in heavenly places might be known, by the church, the manifold wisdom of God'. It is this pride of the bridegroom in his wife; he is proud of her beauty, proud of her appearance, proud of all that pertains to her; and he wants to show her to the family, to all his creatures. That is the sort of relationship that exists between the Lord Jesus Christ and his church. I am extracting the principle out of the details first, because they give us an understanding of this wonderful mystical relationship. And so the picture is of our Lord rejoicing in the relationship, happy in it, triumphant in it, glorying in it. There is nothing that he will not do for his bride, the church.

Such is the first great matter that emerges in the apostle's treatment of this vast and exalted subject. We have to start with this picture of Christ and the church. You see how he looks upon her, and what he does for her because he looks upon her in that way, what he has in view for her—his ultimate objective. And because of all this there is the extraordinary concept of the mystical relationship, the unity, the idea that they are one flesh, and that she is his body. 'Husbands, love your wives, even as Christ loved the church.'

There, then, is our first great principle—Christ loving the church. The relationship between Christ and the church is that which should exist between husband and wife. So start with that. Look at the great doctrine of the church. Come all of you, married and unmarried. This is true of all of us because we are in the church. How wonderful to realize that we are in this relationship to Christ! That is how he looks at you, that is his attitude towards you. The principle is this; this love, this God-like love, is altogether above the erotic and philanthropic which is the highest the world can know. The great characteristic of this love—and this is where it is essentially different from the others—is that this is not so much governed by the desire to have, as by the desire to give. 'God so loved the world.' How? 'That he gave.' There is nothing wrong with the other types of love—I have said this previously—but even when you have them at their best they are always self-centred, they are always thinking of themselves. But the characteristic of this other love is, that it does not think of itself. He gave himself; he died for her 'even unto death'. Sacrifice is the characteristic of this love. This love is a love that gives; it is not always considering what it is going to have, but what it may give for the benefit of the other. 'Husbands, love your wives like that, even as Christ loved the church.'

Having looked thus in general at Christ's attitude towards the church, we can proceed to show how that attitude manifests itself in practice; and then beyond that to its ultimate objective, and finally to the mystical relationship and union. Let us thank God that when we come to consider marriage, which is so common, and apparently so ordinary, we discover, if we are Christians, that we have to consider it in such a way that it brings us into the very centre of Christian truth, into the heart of theology and doctrine, into the mysteries of God in Christ as seen in and through the church. May God bless that consideration to us!

5. The Bride of Christ

Ephesians 5:25-33

THE APOSTLE'S FUNDAMENTAL PROPOSITION, so we have seen, is that we cannot understand the duties of husbands and wives unless we understand the truth about Christ and the church; we have therefore started with that truth, as the apostle does. The husband is to love his wife, 'even as Christ loved the church'. We have reminded ourselves of the content of the word 'love'. It is the highest word that the Bible knows. It is the same sort of love wherewith Christ loved the church; indeed, wherewith God has loved the world. Therefore we are concentrating upon this love of the Lord Jesus Christ for the church. We have only looked at it in general so far. We have looked at his whole attitude towards the church. His concern about her, his pride in her, the way in which he shields her and guards her and protects her. That is brought out here.

But we must proceed beyond that aspect, because the apostle is at pains to remind us that this attitude of Christ toward the church is something which manifests itself in practice. That is the matter we now take up. 'Husbands, love your wives, even as Christ also loved the church, and gave himself for it.' It is not enough to consider his attitude towards the church, the way he looks at the church and regards the church. That is something, says Paul, which has manifested itself in practice. And we must emphasize this, because it is the apostle's emphasis here.

The principle, therefore, is that love is not something theoretical. Love is not something merely to be talked about;

love is not just something to be written about, not something merely about which you write poetry. Love is not merely the theme of some great aria in an opera, or some great song, or this miserable 'crooning', or whatever it is called. Love is not something which you look at theoretically or externally. Love is the most practical thing in the world. That is the great principle we are taught here. There is no word, perhaps, that is being more debased at this present time than the word 'love'. Many people obviously have no idea as to what it means. The world, perhaps, has never used terms of endearment so freely; but there has never been so little love. Everybody addresses everybody else in terms of endearment; the superlatives are all being used. People who scarcely know one another bandy these tender terms about; but there is no content to them. That is why people whom, if you listen to their talk, you would imagine to be the greatest lovers the world has ever known, really know nothing about love and may well be divorced almost the next day. For some reason the idea is widespread that love is something to be talked about, to be sung about. This is where the poets can be so dangerous. Have you ever noticed the extraordinary contrast between the things the poets sing about in their poems, and their actual lives. Is it not tragic that that can be true about men who can write so beautifully and marvellously about love? When you read the biographies of these men you are shocked, you are amazed, and feel the facts are scarcely possible. It is all because they have never understood the meaning of love. They think of it in a theoretical manner, as something very beautiful, but the truth about love is that it is the most practical thing in the world.

Such is the teaching of our Lord himself. 'He that hath my commandments and keepeth them, he it is that loveth me' (*John* 14:21). How prosaic it sounds to us with all our so-called romantic view of love! It is, of course, not romantic at all, it is ridiculous, it is sentimental, it is carnal. 'This is love',

Christ says, 'that a man keep my commandments'. For it is not what you and I say that finally proves whether we are truly manifesting love; it is what we do. This is certainly the essential matter in the relationship between husband and wife. The question is not whether the man can write marvellous letters and use great expressions and protestations of his love; the test of the man's love is his conduct in the home day by day. Not what he was like before they were married, not what he is like on the honeymoon, not what he is like during the first few months of married life. The vital question is, What is he like when there are problems and difficulties, and trials, and illness, and when middle age and old age come along?

Many marriages break down because people do not realize what love means, at the beginning. Remember the apostle's description of it in 1 Corinthians chapter 13, in which he emphasizes its essentially practical character. He tells us that it does not do this, that it does do that; and sums it all up by saying, 'Love never faileth'. That is the test of love! If you want to test whether a man's love to his wife is what it should be, do not listen to what he says, observe what he does, and what he is. That is the test!

The apostle brings all that out here, and he does so in this most amazing manner. 'Husbands, love your wives, even as Christ also loved the church.' How do we know that he loved the church? Here is the answer: 'and gave himself for it'. That is love—'he gave himself for it'. But he does not stop at that.

> Husbands, love your wives, even as Christ also loved the church, and gave himself for it; that [in order that] he might sanctify and cleanse it with the washing of water by the word, that [in order that] he might present it to himself a glorious church, not having spot, or wrinkle, or any such thing; but that it should be holy and without blemish.

Let us look at it carefully and analyse it. There are three strands, surely, in what the apostle says here. This love of Christ, this attitude of Christ towards the church displays itself in practice in three main respects. First, there is what he has already done for the church. Christ loved the church and gave—he has done it—'gave himself for it'. Here, of course, we are at the very heart and centre of Christian truth. There would be no church apart from this. This was the first thing that was absolutely essential; this is the foundation. And so the apostle says, in writing to the Corinthians, 'Other foundation can no man lay'. It is just Jesus Christ and what he has done. That is why he determined not to know anything among them 'save Jesus Christ and him crucified'. There would have been no church at Corinth but for that, nor anywhere else. And, of course, this is a truth which is emphasized everywhere. Call to mind the story of the apostle saying farewell to the elders of this church at Ephesus. You find the account of it in the twentieth chapter of the book of the Acts of the Apostles. He says, 'Feed the church of God, which he hath purchased with his own blood'. That is part of the great romance of Christ and the church, the bride-groom and the bride. He had to buy her before he could have her as his bride. The apostle puts it here in terms of the church as a whole, but let us remind ourselves, and be quite sure of this in our minds, that this is true of every single one of us, every Christian, every member of the church. The apostle does not hesitate to say so in his own case. He says in Galatians chapter 2, verse 20, 'the Son of God, who loved me, and gave himself for me'. Christ loved the church and gave himself for her—yes but also 'for me', for everyone of us as individuals.

The apostle has already introduced this great theme in this very epistle. He did so in the first chapter in verse 7 where he says: 'In whom we have redemption through his blood, the for-giveness of sins, according to the riches of his grace'. It is also the great theme in the second chapter: 'But now in Christ Jesus ye who sometimes were far off are made nigh'—How?—'by the blood of Christ'. 'He is our peace, who hath broken down the middle wall of partition'. He has abolished it. How? 'In his flesh'. 'And that he might reconcile both unto God in one body by the cross, having slain the enmity thereby'—and so on. And, indeed, in this very chapter we are considering, the fifth chapter, he has introduced the same thought in the second verse: 'Be ye therefore followers of God, as dear children, and walk in love, as Christ also hath loved us, and hath given himself for us an offering and a sacrifice to God for a sweetsmelling savour'. He keeps on repeating it; and we must keep on repeating it. Some foolish people say, 'Ah, the cross only applies to my conversion, my original salvation, I then go on . . .' No! Believers never go from this! This is something we should never desire to forget; it is something that continues. It is not only foundation and basis, it is the source of the life and the power that continues—'loved the church, and gave himself for it'.

What Paul is saying then is this—and it is supreme doctrine; there is no higher doctrine—all that the Lord Jesus Christ did, he did for the church. 'Christ loved the church, and gave himself for it'. Our Lord reminds his Father of this in his great high priestly prayer recorded in the seventeenth chapter of John. He puts it in this way: 'Father, the hour is come; glorify thy Son, that thy Son also may glorify thee. As thou hast given him power over all flesh, that I should give eternal life to as many as thou hast given him.' They are his people, they are the church. He says, 'I pray not for the world, but for them whom thou hast given me'. And here we are reminded that he died for the church. We must never lose sight of this. He died for the church; he died for nobody else. His death, as Calvin and other expositors remind us, because it was eternal and because he is the Son of God, is sufficient for the whole world; but it is efficient only for the church. His purpose in dying was to redeem the church. He gave himself for the church, for all who belong to her when she will be complete and perfect and entire. All was known to God from eternity, and the Son came, and gave himself for the church.

What we have to remember, therefore, is that we could never be his at all, and we could never be enjoying any of the benefits of this Christian life, unless he had done this. You and I have to be rescued and to be redeemed before we can belong to the church. Nothing else makes us Christian. Let us remind ourselves of this in passing. You may be the best moral man in the world, but that will never make you a Christian; it will never make you a member of Christ, never make you a member of the church. There is only one thing that puts a man into the church, and that is that Christ has purchased him with his own blood, that he has died for him, redeemed him. This is the only way of entry into the true church—not the visible church, but the true church, the invisible, the spiritual body of Christ. We are saved 'by his precious blood'.

But notice that the apostle's great concern here, particularly, is to emphasize the truth from the standpoint of showing the greatness of Christ's love to the church. Why did he do these things, and how did he do these things for us? We have the answer in many places in the Scripture. How should a husband love his wife? As Christ loved the church and gave himself for it. What did that involve? Perhaps the best statement concerning that matter is in the Epistle to the Philippians, chapter 2, verse 5.

> Let this mind be in you, which was also in Christ Jesus: who, being in the form of God, thought it not robbery to be equal with God: but made himself of no reputation, and took upon him the form of a servant, and was made in the likeness of men: and being found in fashion as a man, he humbled himself, and became obedient unto death, even the death of the cross.

What does that mean? It means that that is how Christ loved the church, and gave himself for it. He did not consider himself. That is the first point. 'He thought it not robbery to be equal with God'; which means that he did not regard his equality with God as a prize to be held on to. He was the eternal Son of God, he had been sharing that glory with his Father and the Holy Spirit from all eternity, but he did not hold on to that and say, 'Why should I go to earth, why should I lay aside the signs of my glory, why should I go down and be buffeted and spat upon?' No! 'He thought it not robbery to be equal with God', he did not regard it as something which he must hold on to at all costs because it was his by right. Instead, 'he made himself of no reputation.' There was no need for him to do so; there was no compulsion at all apart from the compulsion of love. If the Lord Jesus Christ had considered himself, if he had considered his own eternal glory and dignity, there would never have been a church at all. He was the one through whom all things had been created; all the angels worshipped him, and all the great powers and principalities did their obeisance to him. They worshipped him as the Son and glorified him. What if he had said, 'O, I cannot, I cannot put any of that aside; I must have this respect that is due to me, I must have my position.' He did the exact opposite, 'he made himself of no reputation', he was born as a babe in the likeness, the form, of a man. Not only that, he even became a servant. He did not think of himself at all. If he had done so, none of us would have been saved, and there would be no church. He did not talk about his rights; he did not talk about his dues; he did not say 'Why should I suffer, why must I humble myself?' He did not consider the cost, he did not consider the shame. He knew what was to be involved, he knew that he would be buffeted by those Pharisees and scribes and Sadducees and doctors of the law, that people would jeer at him, and throw stones at him, and spit upon him—he knew that all that was to come though he had not done anything to deserve it. Why then did he do it? For the church; because of his love for the church. 'He humbled himself and made himself of no reputation'. He had but one thought, that was the good of the church, the body that was to become his bride. He was buying her, purchasing her, thinking of nobody but her. Not himself, but her! 'Let this mind be in you also', you husbands! 'Husbands, love your wives, even as Christ also loved the church, and gave himself for it.'

But there is another aspect of this which we must emphasize in order to bring out the depth of the teaching. Our Lord did that for us, for the church, while we were yet sinners, while we were ungodly, while we were enemies. Paul's argument in Romans chapter 5 uses these very terms, 'In due time Christ died for the ungodly', 'while we were yet sinners'. 'If, while we were enemies we were reconciled to God by the death of his Son, much more, being reconciled, we shall be saved in his life.' Notice the terms. We were 'ungodly', we were 'enemies', we were 'sinners', we were vile, there was nothing to recommend us at all. You who feel you must read romances, and delight in the story of Cinderella, look at this. Look at the church in her vileness, in her rags, in her sin, in her enmity, in all her ugliness. The Son of God, the prince of glory, loved her while she was like that, and in spite of it; loved her even to the extent of giving himself for her, dying for her. 'Husbands, love your wives, even as Christ loved the church.' We are not called to do what he did to that extent. But he, in spite of everything, loved to that point of giving himself; his blood was shed literally, for us.

'Now', says the apostle,

> you who are in this married relationship find things in each other that you do not like and do not approve of—deficiencies, faults, failures, sins—and you are critical, and stand on your dignity, and condemn, and quarrel, and separate. Why? Simply because you fail to remember the way in which you yourselves have been saved, and have become Christians and members of the Christian church.

He reminds them that if the Lord Jesus Christ had reacted to them as they react to one another there would never have been a church. 'Love never faileth', love goes on loving in spite of everything. That is the love wherewith Christ has loved the church.

Is there anything so wrong, I ask again, as to separate doctrine from practice? How guilty we all are of that! How many of us have realized that we are always to think of the married state in terms of the doctrine of the atonement? Is that our customary way of thinking of marriage—husbands, wives, all of us? Is that how we instinctively think of marriage—in terms of the doctrine of the atonement? Where do we find what the books have to say about marriage? Under which section? Under ethics. But it does not belong there. We must consider marriage in terms of the doctrine of the atonement.

The most foolish of all Christians are those who dislike doctrine, and decry the importance of theology and teaching. And does not that explain why they fail in practice? You cannot separate these things. You must not relegate the doctrine of the atonement simply to your conversion or to the study. Why is it that so many Christian people do not attend an evening service. 'Oh', they say, 'the sermon is going to be about the cross, it is going to be about forgiveness, that is the beginning of the Christian life. I have been a Christian for years now, and of course that has nothing to say to me'. Foolish Christian! Have you got tired of hearing about the cross? Do you know so much about it, do you understand it so exhaustively, that it cannot any longer move you? 'Ah', you say, 'I want the higher teaching now, I want the detailed teaching now as to how I am to live the sanctified life'. You will never live the sanctified life unless you are always there by that cross, and unless it is governing the whole of your life, and influencing the whole of your outlook and your every activity. We are here in what is called the practical section of the Epistle to the Ephesians, the second half, where Paul takes up these ordinary questions; yes, but it is in this very context that he suddenly brings us face to face with the doctrine of the church, and the doctrine of the atonement. You cannot leave the cross behind, you are never such an advanced Christian that that is a mere beginning as far as you are concerned. That is the way to make shipwreck of marriage, and everything else. No! 'Love so amazing, so divine, demands my soul, my life, my all'—always! I start there, but I continue there; and woe unto me if I ever cease to be there!

That is the first point the apostle makes—the love of Christ. But then he goes on to a second point—that which Christ, because of this great love of his, is doing, or continues to do for the church, he puts that in the 'gave himself for it; that he might sanctify and cleanse it with the washing of water by the word' (verse 26). Here is another of these great and most vital statements. Notice that this verse has two main functions. The first is the one I have already mentioned, that it reminds us of what the Lord Jesus Christ is continuing to do for the church. But it has a second object also. It tells us why he did the first thing. 'He gave himself for it; that [in order that]'—this is his object. Why did Christ die? He died 'in order that he might sanctify and cleanse it with the washing of water by the word'. That is the teaching we have here concerning the doctrine of sanctification. It is all here—atonement, justification, and now sanctification.

The first point which we establish and emphasize in this: Forgiveness and deliverance from condemnation, and from hell, are never an end in and of themselves, and must never be considered to be such. They are but a means to a further end. You cannot stop at forgiveness and justification.

Let us take a closer look at what the apostle teaches here about his great doctrine of sanctification. The first principle is that there is nothing which is so utterly unscriptural as to separate justification and sanctification. There are many who do so. They say, 'You can believe on the Lord Jesus Christ as your Saviour, and your sins will be forgiven, and you will be justified. And you can stop at that'. They add, 'Of course you should not do so, you should go on to the second step. But there are many Christians', they say, 'who stop at that. They have believed on Christ unto salvation and they are justified and forgiven; they are certainly Christians, but they have not taken up sanctification'. So then they exhort them to 'take' sanctification as they had previously 'taken' justification. Such teaching is a complete denial of what the apostle says here, and is utterly unscriptural. The death of Christ is not merely to bring us forgiveness, and to justify us, and to make us legally righteous in the sight of God. 'He gave himself for it; that [in order that] . . .' It is only the first move in a series; it is not a last move in any sense, and you can never stop there.

The apostle not only teaches this truth to the Ephesians; he teaches it to all the churches. You find the same in the Epistle to the Romans, chapter eight, verses 3 and 4. It also appears in Titus 2:14: 'He gave himself for us, that he might redeem us from all iniquity, and purify unto himself a peculiar people, zealous of good works'. That is why he gave himself for us; not merely that we might be forgiven, not merely to save us from hell, but to purify and to separate unto himself this peculiar people who are zealous of good works. Our Lord said it all in his high priestly prayer (*John* 17:19): 'For their sakes I sanctify myself, that they also might be sanctified through the truth'.

To stop at justification is not only wrong in thought; it is impossible for this reason, that it is something which Christ does; it is he who does this in us. He gave himself for the church. Why? That he might sanctify and cleanse the church. He is going to do it. The whole trouble arises from the fact that some persist in regarding sanctification as something that we decide to go in for. That is never taught anywhere in the Scriptures. The teaching of the Scripture is this—Christ has set his heart and his affection upon the church. There she is, under condemnation, in her sin, and in her rags and in her vileness! He came, the incarnation had to happen, he took on him 'the likeness of sinful flesh'. He took her sins upon him, and he bore them in his own body on the tree. He has taken the punishment, he has died, he has made atonement, he has reconciled us to God. So the church is delivered from condemnation. But that does not satisfy him. He wants her to be a glorious church, he wants to 'present her to himself a glorious church, without spot, or wrinkle, or any such thing'. So he immediately proceeds to prepare her for that destiny. He cannot stop at the first step; he goes on to sanctify her. In other words, his death upon the cross for us, and our sins, was simply the first step in this great process. And he does not stop at the first step. He has a complete purpose for the church, and he will go through it all step by step.

I would put this very strongly. In the last analysis you and I have no choice in this matter of sanctification. It is something that Christ does. He died for you, and then, having died for you, he is going to wash you, sanctify you, cleanse you—and he will do it. Let there be no mistake about this. If he has died for you he will go on with the process of sanctification in you, he will finally make you perfect. There is something alarming about this; but it is essential biblical teaching. If you and I do not submit voluntarily to this teaching he has another way of cleansing us; and he will use it—'Whom the Lord loveth he chasteneth, and scourgeth every son whom he receiveth' (*Heb.* 12:6). He will not allow you to remain where you were in your filth and vileness, saying 'I am all right, Christ has died for me, I am forgiven, I am a Christian'. He will not have that! He has loved you, you belong to him; and he will make you clean. If you will not come voluntarily, and in the right way, he will put you into that gymnasium of which we read in Hebrews. He will get rid of the corners, he will get rid of the filth and the vileness, he will wash you. It may come about through an illness which he will send upon you. These 'faith-healers' who say that God never sends an illness are simply denying the Scriptures. As one of his methods, he chastises. Your circumstances may go wrong, you may lose your job, or someone dear to you may die. Christian! because you belong to him, because Christ has died for you, he will make you perfect. Fight against him as you will in your folly, he will knock you down, he will cleanse you, he will perfect you. That is the teaching; it is something he does. Sanctification is not something that you and I determine—'He gave himself for it, that [in order that] he might sanctify it and cleanse it with the washing of water by the word'. The first principle therefore which we must grasp is that sanctification is primarily and essentially something that the Lord Jesus Christ does to us. He has his ways of doing it. It includes, of course, obedience on our part. But you must not put your primary emphasis there. The decision for sanctification is not ours; it is his. It was taken in eternity before the foundation of the world. It is his activity, it is his operation; and having died for you, he will do it. Resist him at your peril. He will bring every son who has been called, into that final and everlasting glory. As Hebrews 12 puts it, if he does not deal with you in this way, you are 'a bastard' and not a true son (*Heb.* 12:5-11).

That then is the great principle which forms the basis of this apostolic teaching. How does Christ carry it into effect? The answer is to be found in the word 'sanctify', 'Even as Christ also loved the church, and gave himself for it; that he might sanctify'. This word 'sanctify' is used in many different ways in the Bible, but its primary meaning is, 'to set apart for God, for his peculiar possession and for his use'. You will find, for instance, in Exodus 19 that the mount on which God met with Moses and gave him the Ten Commandments was 'sanctified' in that way. It is called the 'holy mount' because it was set apart. There was no change in the mountain, but it was set apart for God's purpose, for God's use, for God's peculiar possession. The vessels that were used in the temple ceremonial were likewise sanctified, or set apart. There was no material change in the cups and the platters, but as they were to be used in the temple and for God's service only, they could not be turned to common use. To be sanctified means to be set apart for God and for his special use and purposes, as his peculiar possession. So we are 'people for his own possession'.

Then a secondary meaning emerges. Because they are thus set apart they are also 'made holy'. Now here in our passage there can be no question as to the meaning of this word 'sanctification'. It carries that first connotation. 'That he might sanctify it'. It has the meaning of 'set apart for himself', 'separate from everything else, for his own possession, for his own use, for his own delight'. It does not mean more than that here, for we note that the apostle adds the word 'cleanse', supplying the second meaning of sanctify. He divides it up into two steps. Here is the church in her rags, in her filth and vileness! Christ has died for her, he has saved her from condemnation. He takes hold of her where she was and sets her apart for himself. She is 'translated from the kingdom of darkness, into the kingdom of God's dear Son' (Col. 1:13)—that is to say, she is moved out of the world into the special position which, as the church, she is to occupy.

This is a wonderful thing. This is what the Lord Jesus Christ has done with the church. The same occurs when a man finds his affections and his love set upon one girl out of thousands. He chooses her for himself, and he selects her from all the others. 'She is to be mine', he says. So he separates her, isolates her, 'sanctifies' her, puts her there quite on her own. He wants her for himself. That is the simple truth about everyone of us who is a Christian, and a member of the Christian church in a real sense. Had you realized it—that the Lord of glory, the eternal Son of God, has set us apart, has isolated us for himself, that we might be 'a people for his peculiar possession'?

Let me remind you again of the ninth verse in the second chapter of the First Epistle of Peter which states this truth so gloriously. Do you know what is actually true of you at this very moment? 'Ye are a chosen generation, a royal priesthood [kingdom of priests], an holy nation [set apart]'. We are not perfect and sinless, but we are 'an holy nation' in the sense that we are a group, a nation of people set apart. And Peter goes yet further, 'a peculiar people'—'a people for his own personal and peculiar possession' 'that ye should shew forth the praises of him who hath called you out of darkness into his marvellous light'. That is what Christ has done for the church. He has called us out. That is one meaning of the word *ecclesia*—the 'called out ones'. We are called out of the world, put together here to form this body, this bride for Christ. And then Christ proceeds to deal with us.

In other words, to use the language of Peter in that same chapter again, you and I as Christians are now only 'strangers and pilgrims' in this world. Notice how he puts it. 'Dearly beloved, I beseech you as strangers and pilgrims' (verse 11). We do not belong to this world any longer. We have been taken out of it, we have been separated, sanctified. We are only strangers and pilgrims here; we do not belong to that realm as once we did. The Apostle Paul has already said all this at the end of the second chapter of this Epistle to the Ephesians. He says: 'Ye are no more strangers and foreigners, but fellow-citizens with the saints, and of the household of God'. You were strangers to this before, but now you are in this and strangers to that—sanctified, set apart for himself. That, being interpreted, means that the bride is now no longer free to do some of the things she did before, but lives for her husband and he lives for her. The husband does not look at other women, because his bride is the one he has selected, separated, sanctified for himself. That is how Christ looks at the church. That is how a husband should regard his wife. And we, as the bride of Christ, should think of ourselves as no longer free, no longer belonging to ourselves, no longer deciding what we do, no longer belonging to the world.

Let me leave all this in the form of a question. I am addressing Christian members of the church. We shall come to the application to the husbands later. Here is the practical question which I address to everyone who claims to be a believer in the Lord Jesus Christ, to everyone who says, 'I believe Christ has died for me and for my sins, to rescue me'. Are you aware of the fact that Christ has separated you, that he is sanctifying you? Because, believe me, if you are not, you are deluding and fooling yourself in thinking that he has died for you. When Christ dies for an individual he always takes that individual, and moves him (or her), and puts him into this peculiar position. 'He gave himself for it, that [in order that]'—It was the first step in the move; but he never stops at that. That is the preliminary that leads to sanctification. So it is idle to claim that Christ has died for us unless we know that he has separated us. Do you know of a surety that you no longer belong to the world, that there has been a change in you, that you have been moved, that you have been 'translated from the kingdom of darkness into the kingdom of God's dear Son'? Do you feel that you are a stranger here? Do you say with Paul, 'Our citizenship is in heaven'? (*Phil.* 3:20). 'He gave himself for her, that [in order that] he might put her on one side for himself, his own peculiar possession.' O the privilege of being a Christian, of belonging to this company for whom Christ died, and whom he is preparing for himself—set apart from the world for the glory which we are to enjoy with him! Husbands, love your wives in that way.

6. The Purification of the Bride

Ephesians 5:25-33

IN OUR CONSIDERATION of the statement which the apostle makes concerning the duty of husbands towards their wives we are giving attention to the teaching concerning our Lord in his relationship to the church. We have seen his concern for her, his attitude with respect to her; and we are emphasizing how this attitude and concern have expressed themselves in action, in practice. We have seen what the Lord has done for the church—'He gave himself for it'. We have also considered what he is still doing for the church. He has done that first thing once and for ever—he gave himself for it. But he does not leave it at that; he goes on doing something to the church and for the church.

We have been looking also at the word 'sanctify' and its meaning. The Lord has set the church apart for himself; we are his 'peculiar people', a people for his own peculiar, special possession, his bride. He has set her aside and apart in order that he may do certain things for her.

From that point we now proceed. The next word we come to is the word 'cleanse'. 'That he might sanctify and cleanse it with the washing of water by the word.' It is by way of this word 'cleanse' that the idea of purifying—what we normally call 'sanctification'—really comes in.

Here we must be careful to note the full content of this word 'cleanse'. There are some who would confine it solely to our being washed from the guilt of our sins. But that, clearly, is not enough. We have already found that aspect in the statement that he gave himself for the church and separated her. There is implicit in that the idea of our being delivered from the guilt of sin, but I am not disposed however to quarrel with those who want to include it in this word 'cleanse'. Christ certainly cleanses us from the guilt of our sin; but this word takes us still further. I think I can prove that it is not merely a matter of opinion. The very fact that Paul adds that the cleansing is effected 'with the washing of water by the word' is proof that it is a continuous and continuing process. The washing from the guilt of sin is once and for ever. That is a single action; but here is a continuing action, 'That he might cleanse her with the washing of water by the word'. That statement shows that it is not merely a matter of getting rid of the guilt. But then the twenty-seventh verse establishes the matter still more positively—

> That he might sanctify and cleanse it with the washing of water by the word, that he might present it to himself a glorious church, not having spot, or wrinkle, or any such thing; but that it should be holy and without blemish.

These words define Christ's ultimate objective—that the church should not only be delivered from the guilt of sin, but that she should be delivered entirely and completely from sin in every shape and form. Surely Toplady states this idea to perfection when he puts it thus:

> Be of sin the double cure,
> Cleanse me from its guilt and power.

The New Testament never stops at the guilt; it always goes on to this further idea of our being cleansed from the power of sin also. Indeed I want to add even to that. This cleansing is not only from the guilt of sin, and from the power of sin, it is also from the pollution of sin. That third aspect is very frequently forgotten. You will find that many societies in their 'basis of faith' mention the power of sin, but leave out the pollution of sin. Yet in many ways the most terrible thing about the Fall is that it has polluted our nature. Sin is powerful within us very largely because of our polluted nature. This is what the apostle describes so graphically in the seventh chapter of the Epistle to the Romans. 'I know', he says, 'that in me (that is to say, in my flesh) dwelleth no good thing'. Now that is pollution; that is not power. It leads to power; but it is because our natures are polluted, and are tarnished, and are soiled, and made unclean by the Fall, that sin is so powerful within us. Therefore we need to be cleansed not only from the guilt, and not only from the power, but in particular from this terrible pollution of sin—the stain of it all and the perversion.

Sin has entered into the warp and woof of human nature; our very natures are vile and twisted and perverted. How vitally important it is that we should realize that that is true of all of us by nature! It is not that we are neutral by nature, and that we are tempted from the outside. No! we are 'born in sin', we are 'shapen in iniquity'. 'In sin did my mother conceive me'—that is the teaching of the Scripture (*Psa.* 51:5). The apostle has already stated this clearly at the beginning of his second chapter, where he says, 'we were dead in trespasses and sins'—and so on, and he talks about 'the lusts of the flesh and of the mind'. That is another way of describing this 'law within my members'. It is not only a power, it is an infection, it is indeed, as I say, a pollution. It is like a stream polluted at its very source, rather than one which becomes polluted during its course. That is the thing from which we have to be cleansed before we can be presented by the Lord to himself 'as a glorious church, not having spot, or wrinkle, or any such thing; but that it should be holy and without blemish'.

The question for us therefore is—How is this accomplished? The apostle says that it is done 'with the washing of water by the word'. Here we have an important and a very difficult phrase—a phrase which has often been misunderstood and

misinterpreted. There are many who see here the teaching of
what they call 'baptismal regeneration'—that we are delivered
and cleansed entirely from sin by baptism. It was an error
which crept into the church in the first centuries; it is an error
which is perpetuated by the teaching of the Roman Catholic
church, and other forms of Catholicism, even until this present
time. I am not going to enter into all that, because it seems
to me that it is such an utterly artificial interpretation of the
words, imposing a meaning upon them which, taken naturally, and at its face value, they never would have suggested. It
was introduced, of course, in the interests of the power of the
church; and all who still teach it, whatever form of Catholicism
they may claim to have, are still guilty of the same error. The
point here is not some magical action which takes place in baptism, neither is it the particular formula which is used. Some
have emphasized the latter by saying that it is the word spoken
by the man who is baptizing the infant that matters, and that
the formula supplies the efficacious power. Again, that is but
sacerdotalism; it is nothing but a way of bolstering up the authority of a priesthood.

What then does this word teach? Obviously there is a reference here to baptism, to the fact and the act of baptism. That
of course is not surprising, because here we are dealing with
people who were once pagans. They heard the gospel, they
believed it, and then before they were admitted into the church
they had to be baptized; and having been baptized they were
received into the membership of the Christian church. Therefore baptism did stand out in their minds as something which
was meant to represent this cleansing, this deliverance from
one realm and 'translation' into another realm. And so you
find the Apostle Paul putting it thus in writing to the church at
Corinth (*1 Cor.* 6:9-11):

> Know ye not', he says, 'that the unrighteous shall not inherit the king-
> dom of God? Be not deceived: neither fornicators, nor idolaters, nor

adulterers, nor effeminate, nor abusers of themselves with mankind, nor thieves, nor covetous, nor drunkards, nor revilers, nor extortioners, shall inherit the kingdom of God. And such were some of you: but ye are washed, but ye are sanctified, but ye are justified in the name of the Lord Jesus, and by the Spirit of our God.

There again the same idea of 'washing' is used. He says, 'You were like that; you are no longer in that condition; you are now saints in the church—you have been washed'. One of the purposes of baptism is to represent that change.

The Apostle Peter has very much the same thought in his First Epistle, the third chapter, verse 20 and following, he is talking about

the spirits in prison, which sometime were disobedient, when once the long suffering of God waited in the days of Noah, while the ark was a-preparing, wherein few, that is, eight souls were saved by water. The like figure whereunto even baptism doth also now save us (not the putting away of the filth of the flesh, but the answer of a good conscience toward God), by the resurrection of Jesus Christ: who is gone into heaven, and is on the right hand of God.

There, clearly enough, is the idea with which we are dealing in this statement that is before us. Baptism is a figure, and is a representation in symbolic manner, of what the Lord Jesus Christ does for us in this process of sanctification. The object of baptism, therefore, is to represent that, and to seal that to us, to our minds and to our hearts. It does no more. Baptism in and of itself does nothing. Merely to be baptised does not change us as such. That is the false idea of sacraments. The technical term used by the Roman Catholics, and all Catholic teaching, is that sacraments act and are effective *ex opere operato*. In other words, that they act in and of themselves apart from any activity on the part of the recipient—that the very act of baptism makes a child regenerate, or an adult regenerate.

There is no such teaching in the Scripture. Baptism is, as Peter says, 'a figure', a 'like figure whereunto'; it is a dramatic representation. It is the same, of course, with the Lord's Supper. We do not believe that the bread is turned into the very body of Christ. It is a representation. Our Lord says in effect, Look at this bread; when you come to eat it, let that remind you of, let that represent and figure to you my broken body. And likewise with the wine; 'this cup is the new testament'. That is our answer to the Roman Catholics who say that the wine is turned into the blood. They say that we must take these words literally. Well, if you take them literally, what our Lord said was 'This cup'; he did not say, 'This wine', he said, 'This cup is the new testament in my blood', proving that it is simply representative and symbolical.

So it is with baptism. What does baptism represent? Clearly it represents our being washed from the guilt of sin. There we were, sinners, and in sin, under the wrath of God. We have been delivered from that by our faith in the Lord Jesus Christ, by what he has done for us. Baptism reminds us of that deliverance.

Secondly, it reminds us of the fact that we are being cleansed from the power and pollution of sin. It is a sort of 'washing', a symbolical representation of a process of cleansing. It includes that idea also. And thirdly, it stands for the whole concept of our being baptized into Christ by the Holy Spirit. You remember how Paul, in writing to the Corinthians (1 Cor. 10) says that the Israelites were baptized unto Moses by the 'cloud' which was there over them. They were not immersed into the cloud, the cloud was over them. And in the same way baptism represents the fact that we are thus baptized into Christ by the Holy Spirit. That is the whole idea that Paul has in his mind here—our union with Christ. 'We are members', he says, 'of his body, of his flesh and of his bones'. How does that happen? It happens because 'we are baptized by one Spirit into Christ'; baptism stands for that also. So here it is! It is an external symbolical representation

of the three things which the apostle is emphasizing so promi-
nently in this particular section.

Obviously then Paul's main object here is to show us how
Christ is cleansing the church and preparing her for himself;
and that he does so through the Holy Spirit. Clearly it is not
accidental that when our Lord was standing there in the Jordan
at his own baptism, the Holy Spirit came down upon him in the
form and the shape of a dove. So always in baptism we should
be thinking of that aspect, of the coming of the Holy Spirit into
us and upon us in order that he may baptize us into Christ and
proceed with this work and process of sanctification.

So much then for our consideration of the phrase and its
actual terms. It is a very difficult phrase, and it has always
caused a good deal of discussion—'the washing of water'. But
the really important term here is, of course, 'the word'. 'That
he might cleanse it with the washing of water by the word'
or (if you find a change in the order of the phrases helpful),
'That he might cleanse it by the word through the washing
of the water'. The vital thing is this expression 'by the word',
which should be joined to the word 'cleanse'. There is a representation of it in baptism, but it is no more than a representation. The real work of sanctification is done by or through the
Word, and the Holy Spirit does this work in us by means of the
Word. This is a most important truth for Christian people to
grasp and to understand. The instrument which is used by the
Holy Spirit in our cleansing is 'the Word'.

This is the essential New Testament teaching on holiness
and sanctification; it is something which is done in us by the
Holy Spirit using the Word. And let us emphasize that this is
a process. It is a progressive cleansing until we shall be free
from every spot, or wrinkle, or any such thing; free from every
blemish we shall be entirely holy. There are people who teach
that what happens to the Christian is that he is a saved man,
but that he remains in his sin. As long as he 'abides in Christ'

he will be kept from sinning, but there is no change as regards the pollution of sin. That is only dealt with when he comes to die. But that, clearly, according to this teaching, is quite wrong. We read here of a process of cleansing; it goes on. As a man goes on in the Christian life there should be less and less of the pollution of sin in him; he should be becoming progressively sanctified as this process goes on. He is not merely enabled to resist the power of sin, he is being cleansed from the pollution of sin; he is progressively being brought into a state in which he will be finally perfect. And this is done by means of the Word. 'By the Word.'

The great principle which we must lay hold of is that the operations of the Holy Spirit in us are generally in and through 'the Word'. That is why it is always dangerous to separate the Holy Spirit from the Word. Many have done this, and there have often been grievous excesses. Indeed the virtual departure of the people called Quakers from the Christian faith is due to this very thing; they put such emphasis upon the 'inner light' that they ignore the Word. They tend to say that the Word does not matter; it is this inner light that matters. And they have reached the point at which they are more or less detached from New Testament doctrines, and the Lord Jesus Christ is scarcely necessary to their system. And there are others who have emphasized the Holy Spirit to such an extent that they have separated him from the Word. They do not want to be taught, they do not want instruction; they live in the realm of feelings and moods and experiences, and go off into ecstasies that often lead not only to the 'shipwreck of their faith' but to gross immorality and excesses and failures. The Word and the Holy Spirit generally go together. The Word has been given by the Spirit, and he uses his own Word. This is the instrument that he uses. I am not denying that the Spirit can speak to us directly; but I am saying that that is exceptional. And I go further; I say, that anything that we may think is the work of the

Spirit within us must always be tested by the Word. The Holy Spirit will never do anything contradictory to his own Word. So we are exhorted to 'prove the spirits', to 'try the spirits', to 'test the spirits'. Not all spirits are of God; you therefore need a proof and a test of any particular spirit. What provides such a proof? It is the Word. So this work is done by the Spirit, but it is done through and by means of the Word.

Let me further establish this point because it is such a vital one. To show how nearly all the work that the Spirit does in a believer is done by means of the Word, let us start with our regeneration. James puts it in this way: 'Wherefore lay apart all filthiness and superfluity of naughtiness, and receive with meekness the engrafted word, which is able to save your souls'. The Word! Again, James puts it like this: 'Of his own will begat he us with the word of truth, that we should be a kind of first-fruits of his creatures' (*James* 1:21, 18). Peter teaches the same thing—'Being born again', he says, 'not of corruptible seed, but of incorruptible, by the word of God, which liveth and abideth for ever' (*1 Pet.* 1:23). Regeneration is the work of the Holy Spirit, but he does it by the Word—'being born again, not of corruptible seed, but of incorruptible, by the word of God'. It is the Word as used by the Spirit that gives us this new life. Again, take Paul in the First Epistle to the Thessalonians chapter 2 and verse 13:

> For this cause also thank we God without ceasing, because when ye received the word of God which ye heard of us, ye received it not as the word of men, but as it is in truth, the word of God which effectually worketh also in you that believe.

This Word is effectually working in us that believe. It brought us into eternal life, it is continuing to work effectually in us. 'Work out your own salvation, with fear and trembling; for it is God that worketh in you both to will and to do' (*Phil.* 2:12, 13). How does God do so? Through the Word.

Let me give further examples of this self-same thing. Our
Lord himself taught this very plainly and clearly. In the eighth
chapter of John's Gospel you will find an account of how
our Lord was preaching one day, and we are told that when
they heard his words many believed on him. Then we read
this (verse 31): 'Then said Jesus unto the Jews which believed
on him, If ye continue in my word, then are ye my disciples
indeed; and ye shall know the truth, and the truth shall make
you free'. You notice that they have to 'continue in his word',
and if they do so 'the truth shall make them free'. Or listen to
him again in John 15, verse 3: 'Now', he says, 'are ye clean
through the word which I have spoken unto you'. It is the
Word that cleanses. And then there are two examples of it in
the seventeenth chapter of John's Gospel. The first is in verse
17: 'Sanctify them through thy truth: thy word is truth'. He
is leaving his disciples in the world, and the enemy is attack-
ing. He says, 'I pray not that thou shouldest take them out of
the world, but that thou shouldest keep them, [cleanse them,
deliver them] from the evil'. 'Sanctify them through thy truth:
thy word is truth'. And then you notice that tremendous statement where he says: 'And for their sakes I sanctify myself.' He
is talking now about setting himself aside for the death on the
cross. Why is he going to do it? 'That they also might be sanctified through the truth.' This, then, is the great principle that we
find taught everywhere in the New Testament. Christ is cleansing the church through the work of the Holy Spirit whom he
has sent, and who uses this Word in doing the work.

But that leaves us with this vital question: What is this Word
which the Holy Spirit uses? We are to be sanctified by means
of this 'Word'. What is the Word of sanctification? What is
the teaching which leads to our progressive sanctification and
deliverance from the power and the pollution of sin? Here,
again, is a vital point in this whole question of the doctrine
of sanctification; because there is very real danger of our

narrowing down this message concerning sanctification, and confining it to some special teaching or formula about sanctification. We are all familiar with such teaching. There are those who say that sanctification (and this is their own term) is 'quite simple'. They have, they claim, a special message about sanctification and holiness which they say is 'quite simple'. It really just comes to this: 'Trust and obey'; 'Let go and let God'. They say that that is the teaching of the Scripture concerning sanctification. So you will find that they present their teaching quite frequently, not to say generally, in terms of some Old Testament stories about which they can let their imagination run riot. They are only concerned to present this formula, this simple formula, they say, about sanctification. 'It is quite simple, you just cease to struggle and to fight, and just "trust and obey"; you "receive it by faith", believe that you have got it, and you go on.' They say there is no more to be said or done.

But is that true to the Word? Is that 'the Word' that leads to our sanctification? Is sanctification represented anywhere in the Scripture as merely some 'formula' which you devise, and then more or less ignore all the New Testament epistles and their teaching, and find illustrations of this simple process in various narratives in the Old Testament? Surely that is to mutilate the scriptural teaching. What is this Word that teaches us sanctification, and which sanctifies us? The answer is, of course, that it is the whole Bible, the whole of the truth that you find in the Bible or in any one of these New Testament epistles. Why did the Apostle Paul ever write this letter to the Ephesians? He wrote it in order that their sanctification might be promoted. They had believed the truth, as he reminds them in chapter one. But he wants them to grow in grace, he wants them to develop, he wants them to be rid of sin—in its guilt, its power and its pollution. He wants them to see that the objective is that they might be perfect and holy, entirely blameless and without spot; and he writes in order that they might be brought to that point. They must go through this process. The whole of this epistle is about sanctification. This is 'the Word'. It is not some little formula which is 'quite simple' which you just apply, and then you have got 'it'. Not at all! You have to enter into all that you have in this epistle. In other words, the Word by which we are sanctified is the whole of the biblical teaching. It is, in particular, all the great doctrines which are taught throughout the Bible; and it is only as we realize this that we see how that other idea which would narrow down and confine sanctification and holiness teaching to just one little formula is, in the last analysis, an ignoring of most of the Bible.

What is this Word by which the Holy Spirit sanctifies us? First and foremost it is the Word about God. When you are teaching sanctification you do not start with man. But that is how it is commonly done, is it not? They say, Is there any failure in your life? Are you unhappy? Are you being tripped by something? Are you ill at ease? Are you living a defeated life? They start with that. 'Listen', they say, 'you can be delivered from these troubles. All you need to do is to surrender that problem; just give it to the Lord and he will deliver you from it. He will take it out of you, and then all you do is to abide in him, and he will keep you right'. Is not that typical of much sanctification and holiness teaching? It starts with man and his problem—'How can I be made happier?', 'The Christian's Secret of a Happy Life', and so on. But that is not how the Bible teaches sanctification.

How does the Bible teach sanctification? You start by looking up into the face of God! You do not start with man; you start with God. There is no profounder way of teaching sanctification and holiness than simply to teach the doctrines concerning the being, the nature and the character of God! You do not start with yourself and your problems and needs; you start with God. You do not start with your desires, you start with the Almighty — 'Holy, holy, holy, Lord God Almighty'! Is there anything that promotes sanctification and holiness as much as that? The Bible is full of this teaching. Call to mind that great statement about the call of the prophet Isaiah, as it is recorded in chapter 6.

> In the year that king Uzziah died I saw also the Lord sitting upon a throne, high and lifted up, and his train filled the temple. Above it stood the seraphim: each one had six wings; with twain he covered his face, and with twain he covered his feet, and with twain he did fly. And one cried unto another, saying, Holy, holy, holy, is the Lord of hosts: the whole earth is full of his glory. And the posts of the door moved at the voice of him that cried, and the house was filled with smoke. Then said I, Woe is me! for I am undone; for I am a man of unclean lips, and I dwell in the midst of a people of unclean lips: for mine eyes have seen the King, the Lord of hosts.

That is the way in which the Bible teaches holiness and sanctification!

Why are we as we are? Why is there so much failure in our lives and so much sin? The answer is found there; we just do not know God! 'Holy Father', said our Lord, 'the world does not know thee: but I have known thee'. 'Oh,' he said, 'if they had but known thee they would not live as they do, but they do not know thee!' They talk about God and they argue, but they do not know thee! 'Holy Father, the world doth not know thee!' The trouble even with us who are Christians is that we do not know God. Forget about your formulae, forget about yourselves and the thing that is worrying you, the thing that gets you down. That is not your trouble. Your very nature is polluted, and if you get rid of that particular problem you will have something else to fight. The real trouble is that we do not know God. It is the men who have sought God, and the face of God, who have been most holy. What we need primarily is not some experience, it is this knowledge of God, of the attributes of God — his glory, his ineffability, his holiness, his almightiness, his eternity, his omniscience, his omnipresence. If you and I but had the realization that wherever we are, and whatever we do, God is looking at us, it would transform our lives! So the Bible, this Word about which our Lord is speaking, is the Word about God, the 'Holy Father'.

This is New Testament teaching concerning holiness. You start with this first, central, all-controlling doctrine. You see it not only in Isaiah; Ezekiel shows us this same thing. He had this vision of God, and felt the same uncleanness, and fell down. Job, we find, had been talking much about God, and criticizing; but now he sees, and he says, 'Mine eye seeth thee'. He now says 'I will lay mine hand upon my mouth', and, 'I abhor myself and repent in dust and ashes' (*Job* 40:4 and 42:5, 6). Have you heard much teaching about the being and the character of God in your holiness and sanctification meetings? How often have you heard sermons about the nature and the being and the attributes of God? All that is taken for granted. We start with ourselves and our problems, and we want to know how we can get rid of the problems or have some special blessing. The approach is wrong. The Word—'thy Word'— is the essential thing. And it is a Word about God to start with, a revelation of the being and the character of God. 'With the washing of water by the word'.

The same Word also reveals to us our state in sin. It tells us what man was like originally. There is no better way of preaching sanctification than preaching about Adam as he was before the Fall. That is what man was meant to be. How often have you heard sermons about Adam in meetings concerning sanctification and holiness? Or sermons about the Fall, the fall of man and its terrible and terrifying consequences? Sanctification? Read the Epistle to the Romans chapter 5, verses 12 to 21—our being in Adam and our being involved in his sin. There is the root of the problem; and we must understand it well. The Word teaches us about it all. That is New Testament teaching about sanctification—this high doctrine in these epistles, rather than stories about some Old Testament characters which we can use as illustrations for our theory! Sanctification is based on the exposition of the truth—concerning God's hatred of sin, and the punishment that God threatens upon all sin. What next? The Ten Commandments! They establish the fact of sin, they pinpoint it, they focus it, they bring sin home to us—so they are part of this teaching. We do not stop at the 'ten words', but they come in, in order to convince us of our need. The law was a 'schoolmaster to bring us to Christ', a revelation of God's holiness. That is why the fathers used to paint the Ten Commandments on the walls of their churches. The law is not a way of salvation, but it is a way of showing us our need of it, and the continuing need of being cleansed. Next, God's gracious purpose of redemption, the covenant of redemption before the foundation of the world, the Father and the Son and the Holy Spirit together planning man's deliverance. Paul has already told us about it at the beginning of this epistle: 'Blessed be the God and Father of our Lord Jesus Christ'—that is how you start preaching sanctification!—'who hath blessed us with all spiritual blessings in heavenly places in Christ, according as he hath chosen us in him before the foundation of the world; that we should be holy and without blame before him in love'. That is it! And next, all about the person and work of the Lord Jesus Christ himself, all that he has done, and all that he has endured. Indeed there is no better way of preaching sanctification than preaching on the cross, for if I look at the cross, and 'survey' it, I come to this conclusion:

> Love so amazing, so divine,
> Demands my soul, my life, my all.

'Ah but', they say, 'we are concerned now about holiness; we have finished with the beginning of salvation, we have finished with the forgiveness of sins. You do not preach the cross in a holiness convention. Of course not! We are interested now in formulae for sanctification. You do not preach the cross here!' But is there anything so calculated to promote holiness and sanctification as the cross?

> When I survey the wondrous Cross,
> On which the Prince of glory died,
> My richest gain I count but loss,
> And pour contempt on all my pride.

It is because we have never truly seen the full meaning of the cross that we are what we are. That is the cause of our failure and our weakness. We have never realized his love to us. If only we really saw the meaning of the cross! If we but had the experience of Count Zinzendorf who, looking at that picture of the cross, cried out—

> Thou hast done this for me,
> What can I do for Thee?

Looking at that he also said, 'I have one passion, it is Christ and Christ alone'.

This is the Word—all the great doctrines, including also the Holy Spirit, his person, his work, his power. What then? His baptising us into Christ, our union with Christ! Then this doctrine of the church. This is the Word that promotes sanctification. And we must go with all these doctrines up to the doctrine of the second coming. It is here in verse 27: 'That he might present it to himself a glorious church, not having spot, or wrinkle, or any such thing; but that it should be holy and without blemish'. When did you last hear a sermon on the second coming of Christ in a holiness convention? 'But', they say, 'that is wrong. You go to a second advent meeting for that; you do not go to a holiness meeting for the doctrine of the second coming!' Thus you see how we have departed from the Scripture. We have introduced a number of special departments into the life of the church. Holiness? 'You do not need the cross here, you do not need the second advent here; you just need this one thing, "quite simple"!' It is only as I realize his purpose for me in that glorious day which is coming, when he will present the church to himself as a glorious church, not having spot, or wrinkle, or any such thing, that my sanctification is promoted. It is that teaching that urges me to be sanctified.

This is how the apostle John says the same thing: 'Beloved, now are we the sons of God, and it doth not yet appear what we shall be: but we know that when he shall appear, we shall be like him; for we shall see him as he is'. And then 'And every man that hath this hope in him purifieth himself even as he is pure'. (*1 John* 3:1-3). The doctrine of the second coming leads to sanctification, to purification. The Word about which the apostle is speaking here, is the entire Word of the Scripture—every doctrine, the whole of redemption from beginning to end, the entire Bible. 'With the washing of water by the Word.'

Having presented this glorious doctrine, I end with a word of exhortation. Because all this is true, what sort of people should we be? Because all this is true, as Paul has been explaining it, you cannot be as you once were; you must separate yourselves. Go on with your sanctification, 'cleanse yourselves from all pollution of the flesh and of the spirit, perfecting holiness in the fear of God'. 'Cleanse and wash your hands, ye double-minded'—these are the exhortations of the Scriptures. But they all arise from the great doctrines.

So we find here that the process of sanctification which is carried on by the Lord Jesus Christ through the instrumentality of the Holy Spirit whom he has sent, is done by, and in, and through the Word. 'Sanctify them through thy truth; thy word is truth.' And no matter at what point you look at it, it will humble you, and it will lead to your sanctification. But above all, start with God: 'Blessed are the pure in heart, for they shall see God'. Have we any time to waste or to spare? What we need is not to get rid of that little problem in our lives; it is to be ready for the glory. It is as we look into the face of God that we see the need of sanctification, and are shown the way whereby our sanctification can be achieved; and it is the function of the Spirit to do this. He leads us to the Word, he opens the Word to us, he implants it in our minds and hearts and wills. He reveals the Lord to us, and so our sanctification, our cleansing, proceeds from day to day, and week to week, and year to year. And as we shall yet see he will go on with it until the work is completed, and we shall be holy and without any blemish in his holy presence. This is the work which the Lord is continuing to do in his people, in the church.

7. The Marriage Supper of the Lamb

Ephesians 5:25-33

WE ARE STILL LOOKING at this most remarkable statement in which the apostle's primary object is to teach husbands their duties towards their wives; and he does this in terms of the relationship of the Lord Jesus Christ to the church. The apostle passes from one to the other, but we have decided that the better procedure, in order to understand his teaching, is to take them separately. We have considered first of all what he says about the relationship of Christ to the church, in order that, having seen that doctrine in its entirety and fulness, we may then be in a position to apply it to the husbands in their relationship to the wives.

We have considered how our Lord died for the church, gave himself for her, and how, having done that, he proceeds to separate her unto himself (sanctify, put on one side, set his peculiar affection upon the church), that he might cleanse her and continue with this process of spiritual purification.

There are still two expressions to consider in connection with this continuing treatment which our Lord gives to the church. They are the two words found in the twenty-ninth verse, where we read that 'no man ever yet hated his own flesh, but nourisheth and cherisheth it, even as the Lord the church'. Paul does not say that 'in the past he has nourished and cherished the church'; the whole purpose is to show that he goes on doing that work. This is entirely in line with what we have been told about the cleansing, which is clearly a continuing process of sanctification. This nourishing and cherishing is also something that continues, and is not merely an action once and for ever accomplished in the past. That is why those who would confine what we have been dealing with hitherto in verse 26 to a past action only seem to me to be missing the entire run and teaching of this whole section. The death of our Lord is once and for all, but all the rest is continuing, with this ultimate objective in view.

Let us then look at these two words; they are most interesting. 'He nourisheth.' This explains itself. Its essential meaning is that of feeding, providing food, providing nourishment. Christ is concerned about the health and the growth and the development and the wellbeing of his church, so he nourishes her. The apostle has, in a way, been dealing with this theme in the fourth chapter where he expresses it in these terms: 'He gave some, apostles; and some, prophets; and some, evangelists; and some, pastors and teachers'. What for? 'For the perfecting of the saints'; for this process that continues. It is something that keeps going on 'for the work of the ministry, for the edifying'—the building up—'of the body of Christ. Till we all come...'—there is the ultimate objective again! So here, we have another way of saying the same thing, and it is wonderful for us to realize as members of the Christian church that the Lord is thus nourishing the life of the church.

It is an expression of his love for us, and of his care for us, that he provides us with the spiritual food we need. The Bible is given by God, by the Lord Jesus Christ, through the Spirit, as food for the soul. It is a part of his nourishing of us. And all the ministry of the church, as chapter 4 reminds us, is designed for the same end. In other words, there is no excuse for the church when she is ignorant or underdeveloped or weak, or marasmic. There is likewise no excuse for any individual Christian. The Lord himself is nourishing us.

Peter, in his Second Epistle, tells us that 'All things that are needful or necessary for life and godliness have been provided'.

That is what makes the position of the complaining Christian such a serious one. We shall never be able to plead the excuse that there was not sufficient food because we were in a wilderness. The food is available, the 'heavenly manna' is provided; everything one can ever need is here in the Bible. Here is nourishment, concentrated, unadulterated, as Peter again puts it in his First Epistle in the second chapter: 'The sincere [unadulterated] milk of the word, that we may grow thereby'. The Lord has provided it. This is a wonderful thing for us to contemplate—that the Lord is nourishing the church. The husband in his care for his wife works to provide food and all that she needs. Parents take care that their children have the right food, and plenty of it, and at the right time. What concern they show in that respect! The Lord is doing that for us in an infinitely greater way.

How are we responding to it? Do we realize that he is nourishing us? A part of his care is to provide acts of public worship. Public worship is not a human institution, a contrivance of man. It is not something that is run like an institution; and people do not come to the house of God—at least they should not—as a matter of duty. They should come because they realize that they cannot grow if they do not come. They come to be fed, to find food for the soul—'nourishment'. The Lord has provided it. God knows, I do not enter the pulpit because I just choose to do so. If it were not for the call of the Lord I would not be doing it. All I did was to resist that call. It is his way. He calls men, he separates them, he gives them the message, and the Spirit is present to give illumination. All this is a part of our Lord's way of nourishing the church.

Then take the word 'cherisheth'. Here is a word which is only used twice in the New Testament. It is a word that conveys a very definite idea, generally that of clothing. What the child needs above everything is food and clothing. What the bride, the wife, needs is the same. Those are the first two things you think of, the food and the clothing—'cherishing'. But it conveys a further idea, namely that of caring for, looking after, guarding. It is an expression of solicitude. When you nourish and cherish a person you show, by a constant watchfulness a care and an anxiety that he or she should thrive and develop and grow. Such are the ideas that are conveyed here by this term 'cherisheth' which is added to the term 'nourisheth'.

Our chief trouble is that we have no true conception of our Lord's interest in us and his concern about us. That is our fundamental lack, we do not know his love. People are often concerned, and rightly of course, about their love to him; but you and I will never love him until we begin to know something of his love to us. You cannot 'work up' love. You can work up excitement or something carnal, but you cannot work up love. In the case of the church love is always a response, a reaction: 'We love him because he first loved us'. We are helpless until he suddenly shines down upon us the beams of his love; and as we realize that, we begin to love. And we come to realize it in this very practical way of understanding something of what he has done for us, and what he provides for us in 'the nourishing' and 'the cherishing'. The more we see that, and realize it, the more shall we be amazed at it, and the more we shall love him in return.

We must not stop at his work for us at the cross. We begin there, but we see that, having finished that work, he goes on to make all this vast and ample provision for us, and to care for us in providence, in things that happen to us, in leading and guidance. In a thousand and one ways he is nourishing and cherishing the life of the church for whom he died. This does not mean that we forget the cross, or turn our backs on it, but that in addition we realize this further work of his for us.

Why does the Lord do all this? Why did he die for the church? Why this process of sanctification and of cleansing? Why the nourishing and the cherishing? What is it all designed for? The answer is found in the tremendous statement of verse 27: 'That he might present it to himself a glorious church, not having spot, or wrinkle, or any such thing: but that it should be holy and without blemish'. Everything is designed to that end. All we have been looking at is the immediate object, but having in sight that ultimate object. That is the purpose, that is the grand end for which the Lord has done, and is continuing to do, the things we have been considering.

But to get the full force of this expression we must vary the translation a little. The truer translation, surely, is this: 'That he himself might present it to himself'. You have got to introduce an additional 'himself' there. And it is added for this reason, that we are reminded at once that every analogy, even the analogies of Scripture, are inadequate. They are only attempts to give us some glimmer of an understanding of what the truth really is. But no illustration is sufficient. The apostle, here, is illustrating this relationship between Christ and the church in terms of a husband and wife; and yet, at once, we meet something which shows that the analogy is inadequate, and does not go far enough. We all know that the normal procedure is that someone else presents the bride to the bridegroom, the father or a relative or friend. He brings the bride to the bridegroom in the service. Having been helped in all her preparations by others—her upbringing and education and even her clothing and so on—the bride is presented to the bridegroom by someone else. But not so here. Here, he will present his bride to himself. 'He himself might present it to himself'.

This is just another way of emphasizing what is the great theme of the Bible throughout—that the whole of our salvation is of the Lord. It is his doing. He even presents his bride to himself because nobody else can do so, nobody else is adequate to do it. He alone can do it. He has done everything for us from beginning to end, and it will end in his presenting us to himself in all this glory which is here described.

The picture before us, therefore, is that of our Lord and Saviour looking forward to the moment, to the day when he will present the church to himself. And what will she be like? She will be 'a glorious church'—which means a church characterized by glory. Here is a term with which we are familiar, in the individual sense, in the Scriptures. The ultimate destiny of each of us, the ultimate issue of all our individual salvation is glorification—justification, sanctification, glorification. Sometimes it is described as 'redemption', as in the great statement, for instance, in 1 Corinthians 1 verse 30: 'Who of God is made unto us wisdom, and righteousness, and sanctification, and redemption'. That really means 'glorification'. Or as Paul puts it in Romans 8: 'Whom he justified, them he also glorified' (*Rom.* 8:30). That is the end. Or as you have it in the Epistle to the Philippians at the close of the third chapter:

> Our conversation is in heaven; from whence also we look for the Saviour, the Lord Jesus Christ: who shall change our vile body (or the body of our humiliation) that it may be fashioned like unto his glorious body (the body of his glorification) according to the working whereby He is able even to subdue all things unto himself.

This is to happen to us individually; but the church also, as a whole, is to be glorified.

That is what is meant by the phrase 'glorious church'. She will be in a state of glory. The apostle helps us to understand it first by describing what she is like externally. He describes this in terms of two negatives. The church, in her glory, will have neither spot nor wrinkle upon her. There will be no stain, there will be no blemish. It is very difficult for us to realize this. While the church is walking in this world of sin and shame she gets bespattered by mud and mire. There are therefore stains and spots upon her. And it is very difficult to get rid of them. All the medicaments that we are familiar with, all the means of cleansing are inadequate to remove these spots and these stains. The church is not clean here; though she is being cleansed, there are many spots upon her still.

But when she arrives in that state of glory and of glorification she will be without a single spot; there will not be a stain upon her. When he presents her to himself, with all the principalities and powers and the serried ranks of all the potentates of heaven looking on at this marvellous thing, and scrutinizing and examining her, there will not be a single blemish, there will not be a spot upon her. The most careful examination will not be able to detect the slightest speck of unworthiness or of sin. The apostle has already introduced us to this idea in chapter 3 and verse 10, where he says: 'To the intent that now unto the principalities and powers in heavenly places might be known by the church the manifold wisdom of God'. These principalities and powers will be looking on; and he, in his pride, will not only present her to himself, but before them. The bride and bridegroom will stand before the hosts of eternity, and he will invite their inspection. He will ask them to look at her, and they will not be able to find a stain or a single spot or blemish upon her—'without spot'.

Yes, and thank God, 'without wrinkle'—'not having spot or wrinkle'. Wrinkles, as we all know, are a sign of age, or a sign of disease, or a sign of some sort of constitutional trouble. Wrinkles are a sign of imperfection. As we all get older we develop wrinkles. The fat disappears from the skin. Disease too can deprive us of this layer of fat, and so it can make us look prematurely old. It does not matter what the cause is—any kind of trouble or anxiety leads to wrinkles. It is all a sign of strain and of decay, of advancing age and failure. The church in this world has many wrinkles upon her; she gets to look old and aged. But, thank God, Paul says, when the great day comes on which Christ will present the church to himself in all her glory, not only will there not be a single spot, there will not be a wrinkle left. Everything will be smoothed out, her skin will be perfect, whole and rounded. It is impossible to describe this perfection. The whole idea is, in a sense, suggested in Psalm

110, where the psalmist looking forward prophetically is given some glimpse of this state of perfection: 'Thy people', he says in the third verse, 'shall be willing in the day of thy power, in the beauties of holiness from the womb of the morning; thou hast the dew of thy youth'. The church will have renewed her youth. Dare I put it like this? The beauty-specialist will have put his final touch to the church, the massaging will have been so perfect that there will not be a single wrinkle left. She will look young, and in the bloom of youth, with colour in her cheeks, with her skin perfect, without any spots or wrinkles. And she will remain like that for ever and for ever. The body of her humiliation will have gone, it will have been transformed and transfigured into the body of her glorification.

This is what we are told in general here about the church. But let me remind you again that in Philippians 3, verses 20 to 21, Paul tells us that the same thing is going to happen to us individually. This is a wonderful thing to contemplate. These bodies of ours individually, yours and mine, are going to be glorified. No infirmities will remain, no vestige of disease or failure or sign of age; there will be a grand renewal of our youth. And we shall go on living in that eternity of perpetual youth, with neither decay nor disease, nor any diminishing of the glory which belongs to us. That is what the church is going to look like externally. Do not forget that the idea the apostle is anxious to convey is this, the pride of the bridegroom in his bride. He is preparing her for 'the Day'. There is going to be his great celebration; he intends to show her to the whole universe.

But not only will that be true of her externally, she will be the same internally. Psalm 45 in a most remarkable manner is a perfect prophetic description of all this: 'The king's daughter is all glorious within'. The psalmist is not content with saying that 'her clothing is of wrought gold' and that 'she shall be brought unto the king in raiment of needlework', he emphasizes that she shall be 'all glorious within' also.

The apostle brings that out here—'but that it should be holy, and without blemish'. She will be positively holy. The apostle's declaration is essentially positive. The holiness, the righteousness of the church is not the mere 'absence' of sin and sins; it is the sharing of the Lord's own righteousness.

This is where the merely moral men are left without any understanding at all. They have no conception of anything but a negative morality; morality to them means that you do not do certain things. That is not what the Bible means by righteousness; the biblical term means 'to be like God'! God is holy, and the church becomes holy with this positive shining righteousness, this perfection. It is much more than a mere absence of evil. It is essentially positive uprightness, truth, beauty, and everything that is glorious in all its essence as it is in God. The church partakes of that. She is clothed with the righteousness of Christ now. Thank God, he sees that, and not us! But, then, there will be more than that. She will indeed be like him, positively, entirely holy and righteous.

And then, to make sure that we understand it, the apostle says, 'without blemish'—which means 'without blame'. He has already said all this in verse 4 of the first chapter:

> Blessed be the God and Father of our Lord Jesus Christ, who hath blessed us with all spiritual blessings in heavenly places in Christ: according as he hath chosen us in him before the foundation of the world.

What for? 'That we should be holy and without blame before him in love.' There was the overture, as it were. You always get the leading themes in the overture. Paul has now taken up that theme which he just mentioned there; here in the fifth chapter he works it out more fully. The church, then, is going to be in this glorious state.

Let me sum it up in the following way. The terms used by the apostle are designed to convey perfection of physical beauty, health and symmetry, the absolute perfection of spiritual character.

Think of the most beautiful bride you have ever seen. Multiply that by infinity, and still you do not begin to understand it. But that is what the church is going to be like. There is never any perfect beauty in this world. A beautiful face, perhaps, but ugly hands. There is always something, some sort of blemish, is there not? But there will be none there. And that is, I suppose, the supreme quality of this beauty that is being described—its symmetry, its absolute perfection in every respect.

This is the thing, surely, we should long for most of all. We are all so lop-sided. Some people are full of head knowledge, the theoretial knowledge of doctrine, and they never move any further. Others have no doctrine, but they talk about their activities and about their lives—they are equally defective. A man who has only a theoretical understanding of these things, and who does not show their power in his life is a very unworthy representative of his Lord. And so is the other! The practical man, so-called, has no time for doctrine, the other has nothing but doctrine: they are both equally at fault. Thank God for a day which is coming when we shall be complete and entire with nothing lacking, and proportionate, balanced. Oh, the glory of this beauty which is here described, and for which our blessed Lord and Saviour is preparing us day by day, week by week, month by month, and year by year! I speak to Christians. Had you realized this about yourselves? Had you realized what a privilege it is to be members of the Christian church? This is what it means to be a Christian! You who are so ready to run to your beauty parlours, do you run to Christ's beauty parlour? That is what the church does. Have we a real understanding of the church as the bride of Christ for whom he has died, and for whom he is continuing to do all these things? Do you know that he cherishes you? Do you know that your name is written in his heart, as well as written upon his very hands? He has loved us with an everlasting love, he has died for us, he has set us apart for himself, he has made all this provision for us, in preparation for that great day when he will present us to himself a glorious church not having spot, or wrinkle, or any such thing, but that we should be holy and without blemish.

This is the process that is going on. And let me remind you again that it will go on until it is finished. Nothing can stop it, nothing will be allowed to stop it, because she is his bride. And if I may venture on such an anthropomorphism, his pride in himself and in her is such that he cannot allow anything to stop the work or to hinder it! It is going on, I say; and it will go on. Here is the biblical guarantee. The apostle has given it already in chapter 3, in verses 20 and 21: 'Now', he says, 'unto him that is able to do exceeding abundantly above all that we ask or think, according to the power that worketh in us, unto him be glory in the church by Christ Jesus throughout all ages, world without end'. That is the power that works in us, and will continue to work. He did not stop at his death; he does not stop at justification; he is continuing to work within us. He does all the apostle has been describing in order that 'Unto him be glory in [and through], the church throughout all ages, world without end'.

That power is irresistible. I would therefore issue this warning once more. If you are indeed a child of God and a member of the church, a member of the body of Christ, let me warn you, in the light of this exalted and glorious teaching, that this body is going to be made perfect, and will be made perfect. Do not resist him therefore, do not resist the ointments, the emollients, the gentle teaching which he gives in his instruction in the Word in various other ways. Because, believe me, if you become deeply stained with sin, he has some very powerful acids that he can use, and which he does use, in order to rid you of the sin! 'Whom the Lord loveth he chasteneth, and scourgeth every son whom he receiveth.' We are accustomed when we come to the communion table to remember what the apostle says about this in 1 Corinthians 11:28-32. 'Let every man', he says, 'examine himself.' The argument is this, that if we do examine ourselves and judge ourselves, we shall not be judged; but if we fail to do so he will do it to us, he will do it for us. There is no question about this; this is quite categorical: 'Let a man examine himself, and so let him eat of that bread, and drink of that cup. He that eateth and drinketh unworthily'—which means in a careless manner, not thinking about what he is doing. Oh yes, he may think a little about Christianity on Sunday, but forget it for six days of the week, then come to a communion service because he is a church member. If you do it in that way, says the apostle, beware: 'Let a man examine himself, and so let him eat of that bread, and drink of that cup. For he that eateth and drinketh unworthily, eateth and drinketh damnation to himself'—and 'damnation' means judgment—'not discerning the Lord's body.' He does not understand what he is doing. 'For this cause'—because they do not examine themselves, because they do not realize that the church is the bride of Christ and that he is going to make her perfect and glorified—'for this cause many are weak and sickly among you, and many sleep'. 'Many are weak' means, never feeling quite well, they do not understand why. 'And many are sickly', that is to say, they are positively ill. 'For this cause'—because they do not examine themselves, the Lord has that other way of doing it. Read the biographies of the saints and you will find that many of them thank God, as they look back, for an illness which came to them. To me, one of the best examples of this is the case of the great Dr Thomas Chalmers who would probably never have been an evangelical preacher if he had not had an illness that kept him on his back in bed for nearly twelve months. That was God's way of bringing him to see the truth fully. 'For this cause many are weak and many are sickly among you'—Yes—'and many sleep'—which means that they are dead. It is a great mystery, I do not pretend to understand it, but the teaching of the apostle is plain and clear.

He says, 'If we would judge ourselves' — if we would examine ourselves and deal with ourselves and punish ourselves — 'we should not be judged. But when we are judged' — What does it mean? — 'we are chastened of the Lord, that we should not be condemned with the world'.

All that, being interpreted, means just what I am trying to say that because the church is the bride of Christ, and because his ambition for her makes him look forward to that great day when she will be 'a glorious church, not having spot, or wrinkle, or any such thing', but she shall be 'holy and without blame before him in love', he carries on his work to that end. And if we do not respond to him, and yield to his endearments and to the manifestations of his tender love and wooing, I assert in his name, that he loves you so much that he will cleanse you, he will bring you there. He may have to apply to you the acid of 'weakness', or the acid of 'sickness' but it will be for your good. Do not misunderstand me. This does not mean that every time we are ill it is of necessity a chastisement. The Scripture does not say that; but it does say that it may be. That has often happened. You can read many instances of it in Scripture. Paul realized that the thorn in the flesh was given him in order to keep him humble lest he be exalted over-much (2 *Cor.* 12:7-10). There are foolish and glib people who say that it is never the Lord's will that a man should be ill. The Scripture teaches that 'the Lord chasteneth whom he loveth', and this is one of his ways — 'many are weak and many are sickly among you, and many sleep'. If you really are a child of God, be careful, be wary. Because you belong to the body of which he is the head, he will cleanse, he will perfect you, he will have you to become that which he has destined for you.

That leaves us with one final question. When is all this going to happen? There seems to be no doubt about this. It must be a reference to the 'second coming' of our Lord himself. It is when he will come and take the church to be with himself.

That is the teaching of the Scripture. 'I go to prepare a place for you. And if I go and prepare a place for you, I will come again, and receive you unto myself; that where I am, there ye may be also'.

In the high priestly prayer recorded in John 17 we have exactly the same teaching. Christ's will is that the church may see 'the glory which I had with thee [the Father] before the foundation of the world'. That is what you and I, as Christians, are going to see. 'We shall see him as he is'. He now has again the glory which he shared from eternity with the Father. He laid aside the signs of that glory when he was here on earth. That is why I never approve of any attempt to paint pictures of our Lord. It is pure imagination, and almost certainly wrong. There are no facts concerning his physical appearance. Scripture is silent at this point. He was here 'in the likeness of sinful flesh', and there is that suggestion in the eighth chapter of John's Gospel verse 57, that he looked much older than he was. He said of himself: 'Before Abraham was, I am'. And they said, 'What is he talking about? He is not yet fifty years old'. He was about thirty-three years old but they chose the figure fifty. That matters little—what does matter is that when he ascended to heaven the glory returned, and he is now in his glorified state. Paul had a glimpse of him, on the road to Damascus, in all his glory. It was so wonderful that he fell blinded to the ground. But you and I are going to see it, to 'see him as he is'. We shall need to be glorified before we can stand that sight; but it will most certainly happen to us. 'And I shall see him face to face.' As the bride of Christ we shall be there by his side sharing this glory.

When is this to be? It is when everything shall have been completed, when the fulness of the Gentiles, and of Israel, shall be saved and the church is complete and entire. There will not be a single person missing or lacking, not one. The devil cannot frustrate this; he is already a defeated foe. The apostle always delights in saying this. He says it gloriously in the Epistle to the Philippians chapter 1, verse 6: 'Being confident of this very thing, that he which hath begun a good work in you will perform it until'—until when?—'until the day of Jesus Christ'. That is the day, 'the day of the Lord', 'the day of Jesus Christ', 'the day of Christ', 'the crowning day [which] is coming by and by'. Or as he has put it at the end of the third chapter of that epistle: 'Our conversation is in heaven; from whence also we look for the Saviour, the Lord Jesus Christ: who'—when he comes—'shall change our vile body, that it may be fashioned like unto his glorious body, according to the working whereby he is able even to subdue all things unto himself.' Nothing can stop it! Again, the apostle, in writing to the Romans in chapter 8 and in verses 22 and 23, says, 'We know that the whole creation groaneth and travaileth in pain together until now. And not only they, but ourselves also, which have the first-fruits of the Spirit, even we ourselves groan within ourselves, waiting for the adoption'—What is that?—'to wit, the redemption'— the glorification—'of our body'. That means getting rid of the spots and the stains and the wrinkles and every such thing, and being entire and glorious in his presence.

Have you noticed this in the 19th chapter of the Book of Revelation, verses 6 to 9?

> And I heard as it were the voice of a great multitude, and as the voice of many waters, and as the voice of mighty thunderings, saying, Alleluia: for the Lord God omnipotent reigneth. Let us be glad and rejoice, and give honour to him; for the marriage of the Lamb is come, and his wife hath made herself ready. And to her was granted that she should be arrayed in fine linen, clean and white: for the fine linen is the righteousness of saints. And he saith unto me, Write, Blessed are they which are called unto the marriage supper of the Lamb.

Oh, the privilege of being invited to the marriage supper of the Lamb, when he presents the bride to himself! She will be clothed with this garment of righteousness without, and within she will be perfect. Oh, the blessing of being present at that marvellous wedding feast! It is not surprising that Jude ends his short epistle by saying, 'Now unto him that is able to keep you from falling, and to present you faultless before the presence of his glory with exceeding joy, to the only wise God our Saviour, be glory and majesty, dominion and power, both now and for ever'.

How should we be feeling? We should feel exactly as any woman who becomes engaged to be married feels. We should be looking forward to the great day, and longing for it, and living for it. This should be at the centre of our lives to the exclusion of everything else. We should be animated by this, stimulated and moved by it, and ever looking forward to it— the wedding day, the ceremony, the friends looking on, the feasting, the wonder and the glory and the splendour of it all!

'That he might present her to himself a glorious church, not having spot or wrinkle, or any such thing, but that she should be holy and without blemish'. He looking into her eyes, she looking into his eyes! That was our blessed Lord's object when he came on earth and lived and died and rose again. It is his objective for us. He died for us that we might come to that! He has separated us that we might come to that! He is cleansing us that we might come to that! He nourishes us that we might come to that! He cherishes us that we might come to that! May God give us grace to realize the privilege of being a member of the Christian church! May we also be given grace and strength and understanding so to realize something of that glory that awaits us that we shall set our affections on that, and not on things on the earth!

8. One Flesh

Ephesians 5:25-33

WE ARE STILL CONSIDERING THE DOCTRINE of Christ's relationship to the church. But it does not end even at what we have seen. We have to go further; and we shall find that the apostle's doctrine rises to still greater heights. You would have thought that there could be nothing more exalted than that twenty-seventh verse where we are given a glimpse of what is awaiting us as the bride of Christ, as members of the Christian church. But the doctrine goes even further; there is something still more wonderful, and almost incredible; and that is the extraordinary doctrine of the mystical union between Christ and the church. The apostle's argument is that we do not truly understand what marriage means until we understand this doctrine of the mystical union of Christ and the church. We shall find that each of the doctrines helps to throw light upon the other. The mystical union between Christ and the church helps us to understand the union between husband and wife, and the union between husband and wife in turn gives a certain amount of light on the mystical union between Christ and the church. That is the wonderful thing about this whole statement. Human analogy and illustration help us to understand divine truth, but in the last analysis it is the understanding of divine truth that enables us to understand everything else; so the apostle passes from one to the other.

We must therefore address ourselves to this exalted doctrine of the union between Christ and the church. We are all no doubt comforted by what the apostle says in verse 32, 'This is a great mystery'. It is indeed a great mystery. Therefore we must approach it with care, and we must also approach it very prayerfully. It is certain that apart from the anointing and unction which the Holy Spirit alone can give, we shall not be able to understand it at all. To the unregenerate, to the unconverted, to the world, this is sheer nonsense; and that is what the world says about it. Even to the Christian it is a great mystery. But, thank God, the use of the term 'mystery' in the New Testament never carries the idea that it is something which cannot be understood at all. 'Mystery' means something that is inaccessible to the unaided human mind. It does not matter how great that mind may be. The greatest brain in the world, the greatest philosopher, if he is an unregenerate man, is not merely a tyro, he is less than a babe, indeed he is dead in a spiritual sense. He has no understanding whatsoever of a subject like this. This is spiritual truth, and it is only understood in a spiritual manner. The best comment on all this is, once more, the First Epistle to the Corinthians chapter 2, verse 6 to the end of the chapter. It is not surprising therefore that such an elevated subject has been frequently misunderstood, and misunderstood in a very drastic manner.

Take, for instance, the teaching of the Roman Catholic church at this point. The Roman Catholic church translates the word which the Authorized Version renders as 'mystery' by the word 'sacrament'. They read, 'this is a great sacrament', and it is from this statement that they elaborate their doctrine that marriage is one of the seven sacraments. They speak about 'seven sacraments'—not merely the two which all Protestants recognize, namely, baptism and the Lord's Supper—and of these marriage is one. Their supposed proof of that is this verse. On such a foundation they introduce their notion of marriage as a sacrament which therefore, of course, can only be performed by a priest. It is just one illustration of the way in which they elevate the priesthood and introduce a magical element into Christianity. It is all designed to do that. But it shows how the Scriptures can be perverted and misused and misappropriated in the interests of a controlling theory from which you start. If you start by exalting your church and the priesthood, then you have to hedge it round and about in every way you can—and that is what they proceed to do. 'Extreme unction' again is something that can only be administered by a priest, so that is a sacrament; and so on. All these things are designed to bolster up this purely artificial power of the priest. I am adverting to this simply to show how a statement like this can be misinterpreted. What shows, finally, how entirely and completely wrong that Roman Catholic interpretation is, is what the apostle goes on to say in this self-same verse—'but I speak concerning Christ and the church'. That is the mystery to which he is referring. It casts its light upon human marriage between a man and a woman, but he is talking about 'Christ and the church'. So the real mystery is the relationship between Christ and the church. Hence the Roman Catholics are really committed to believing that the relationship between Christ and the church is a sacrament. But they do not say that, because it would be folly for them to do so. However, that is one of the ways in which this matter can be entirely misunderstood.

Rejecting the Romanist's view, let us look again at this phrase: 'This is a great mystery'. Paul means that it is a very profound matter; a matter which will call upon all your resources, and which shows the need of what he has already prayed for on behalf of these people in chapter 1—'That the eyes of your understanding might be enlightened' by the Holy Spirit. If we do not approach it thus, anointed by the Spirit, there are three main dangers that will confront us. The first is not to consider it at all. And that is the position, alas, of many Christian people. 'Ah', they say, 'this is a difficult matter', and because it is difficult they do not attempt to understand it, and rush on to the next statement. Surely there is no need for us to stay with that attitude. It is something which can never be defended, and must never be done. The mere fact that there are difficulties in the Scripture does not mean that we should bypass them. They are there for our learning and instruction; and however difficult they may be, we must do our utmost to understand them and to grasp them. That is one of the reasons for the existence of the Christian church. That is why the Lord has given 'some, apostles; some, prophets; some, pastors; some, evangelists; some, teachers'; and so on. It is in order to instruct us in these things; and so that we may grapple with them. We must not say, 'Ah, this is too difficult', and rush on to something else. You will never understand your own marriage, if you are married, unless you try to understand this. It was in order to help you to understand that the apostle wrote this.

The second danger is so to deal with it as to do away with the mystery, or to detract from the mystery. There have been many, including commentators, who have done so. They have been so much afraid of this 'mystical union', and this teaching about it, that they have reduced it to a mere matter of general likeness, a mere unity of interests, and so on. But that is to take the 'mystery' right out of it. They say, 'This is just hyperbole, it is highly dramatic language used by the apostle'. But that is to ignore the fact that Paul deliberately tells us that it is 'a great mystery'. We must not reduce the 'mystery', we must not make something ordinary of it. This is a danger that confronts us at many points in the Christian life, and in Christian teaching. It is the danger that confronts us in connection with our two sacraments—that in our fear of saying too much we say too little! We must avoid that danger.

The third danger is the danger of attempting to work out all this in too much detail. Deciding that it is our duty to face the matter and to try to understand it, and to work it out, we so work it out that there is no mystery left at all. Obviously that is equally wrong, because the apostle himself says, 'This is a great mystery'. That does not mean, I say, that we do not understand it at all, but it does mean that we do not understand it perfectly, that we do not understand it entirely, that there is still something that eludes us, something that leaves us gasping with astonishment and amazement.

Let us then try to avoid these particular pitfalls as we face this great mystery. This is a wonderful truth; and we rise here to those rarified heights which are to be found alone in the Scripture.

What is the apostle's teaching about this mystical relationship between Christ and the church? We can start with something with which we are quite familiar, because we have met it before in this epistle. The first thing he tells us is that the church is the 'body' of Christ: 'So ought men to love their own wives as their own bodies' (verse 28). Then he adds in verse 29: 'No man ever yet hated his own flesh; but nourisheth and cherisheth it, even as the Lord the church'. And then more particularly: 'We are members of his body'. He has already introduced this teaching at the end of chapter 1 and again in chapter 4, verse 16. But the apostle is careful to remind us of this because he is anxious to bring out the principle of the intimate character of the relationship. It is the relationship between the head and the members of a body. What he is concerned to emphasize is that the relationship between husband and wife is not a mere external relationship. There is an external relationship, but much more than that. The essential characteristic of marriage is not simply that two people live together. That is only the beginning; much lies beyond; and there is something deeper here, something much more wonderful. The church, Paul says, is really a part of Christ. As the members of the body are a part of the body, of which the head is chief part, so Christ is the head of the church. As Paul puts it at the end of chapter 1, 'And hath put all things under his feet, and gave him to be the head over all things to the church, which is his body, the fulness of him that filleth all in all'. And again, in the fourth chapter:

> Speaking the truth in love, may grow up into him in all things, which is the head, even Christ: from whom the whole body fitly joined together and compacted by that which every joint supplieth, according to the effectual working of the measure of every part, maketh increase of the body unto the edifying of itself in love.

We must hold on to that principle, as it is an essential preliminary to an understanding of the doctrine of the mystical union.

But that is only introduction. He goes further, and in verse 30 he adds, 'For we are members of his body'—then he makes this extraordinary addition—'of his flesh, and of his bones'. He is talking about the relationship of the church to the Lord Jesus Christ. It is here that we really enter into the mystery. The notion of the church as the body of Christ, while difficult, is nothing like so difficult as this addition, 'of his flesh, and of his bones'. Some have tried to avoid this altogether by pointing out that in certain manuscripts this addition is not present; but it is generally agreed by all the best authorities that in all the best manuscripts this is present. So we cannot solve the problem in that fashion. And indeed the whole context, and the following quotation from Genesis 2, make it essential that we should keep it here, otherwise there is no point or purpose in the quotation. There, as I shall show, he is clearly referring to Genesis 2; and he is certainly doing the same here.

Here we enter into the very heart of this mystery. We must bear in mind that the apostle's intent, his purpose, is still the same. There is the danger, if he just leaves it at saying that the church is the body of Christ, that we may still think of it in terms of some loose attachment. We must not, of course, do that, because anyone who knows anything about the body knows that it does not consist of a loose attachment of a number of parts. It cannot be repeated too frequently that the body does not consist of a number of fingers stuck on to a hand and a hand stuck on to a forearm, and so on. No! The essential thing about a body is the vital organic unity. And it is in order to emphasize, and to safeguard that principle that the apostle makes the addition, and says, 'We are members of his body, of his flesh, and of his bones'.

The only way to solve the problem, it seems to me, is to follow the hint that is given us by the apostle himself, and go back to the statement which he quotes from the second chapter of the Book of Genesis, verse 23: 'And Adam said'—referring to the woman—'This is now bone of my bones, and flesh of my flesh'. Here, again, is a statement that has been misinterpreted. There are those who say that the apostle, in this thirtieth verse of this fifth chapter of Ephesians, is referring to the incarnation, that it is just a round-about way of saying that when the Lord Jesus Christ came into this world he took upon him human nature, that he took upon him, in other words, our flesh and our bones. But such an interpretation is quite impossible. What the apostle is saying is not that the Lord Jesus Christ, the second person in the blessed Holy Trinity, has taken 'our' flesh and bones; what he says is that 'we' take his flesh and bones, that 'we are members of his body, of his flesh, and of his bones'. It is the other way round; so that is not the explanation.

Then there has been grievous misunderstanding of this in terms of the sacrament of the Lord's Supper. There are those who have said that when the apostle writes, 'We are members of his body, of his flesh, and of his bones', he is referring to our Lord's glorified body. The body which the Lord Jesus Christ took unto himself has been glorified, and they say that we are literally parts and members of his glorified body. But surely there is one consideration that puts that out, once and for ever, namely that that glorified body is in heaven. That, therefore, cannot possibly apply to us. But even further, as I say, they have introduced the whole question of the communion, of the Lord's Supper. The Roman Catholics say that there is no difficulty about this. Their teaching is that at the communion table the priest performs a miracle, he turns a piece of bread into the very 'flesh and bones' of the Lord Jesus Christ. That is the doctrine of transubstantiation. What is on the plate looks like bread, but that is only the 'accident', the 'substance' has been changed. The whiteness remains, but what is offered to the communicant is now actually the body of Christ. So that as you eat you are eating 'his flesh and his bones', and so you become a part of him. They drag in the teaching in the sixth chapter of John's Gospel in their attempt to support this.

Then the Lutheran doctrine, which is not transubstantiation, but what they call 'consubstantiation', comes to very much the same thing. They say that the bread is not actually changed into the body of Christ, but the glorified body of Christ enters into the bread, and is there with it. So you have the bread plus the glorified body of Christ, and you eat both.

It should surely be evident that this is merely to import something that is in no way suggested by the apostle, either in the verse itself, or in the entire context. It is an attempt to explain the mystery in a manner which is not consistent with the context; and, in the last analysis, it almost does away with the mystery.

Surely if we follow the apostle's own leading we shall arrive at the true explanation. He is obviously quoting Genesis 2:23: 'Adam said, This woman is now bone of my bones, and flesh of my flesh'. His analogy is clearly that of Adam and Eve, and Christ and the church. So it is right to say of the church that 'we are members of his body, of his flesh, and of his bones'.

But what does that suggest? We must go yet further into the mystery. Is not this like walking into some cave where you see the first chamber, and then see that there is another opening

out of it? You go on into that and on, and on; and in the
most central chamber there is the final treasure. What does
the apostle mean? That depends on the meaning of Genesis
2:23. The answer is, clearly, that the woman has been taken
out of man. Have you noticed the exact wording of Genesis
2:23? 'Adam said, This is now bone of my bones, and flesh of
my flesh: she shall be called Woman'. But why should she be
called 'Woman'? The answer given is, 'because she was taken
out of Man'. The true definition of a woman therefore is one
who has been taken out of man. That is the very meaning of
the word 'woman' . Woman by definition, by origin, by name,
is one who is taken out of man. But observe again the way in
which this was done. 'And the Lord God said, It is not good
that the man should be alone; I will make him an help meet
for him' (verse 18). Again we are told at the end of verse 20,
'but for Adam there was not found an help meet for him'. The
animals had been made, and animals are very wonderful, but
not one of them is a help meet for man. There is an essential
difference between man and the animal. Man is a special creation after all, he has not evolved out of the animals. The animal
at its best is essentially different from the lowest type of man;
he belongs to a different order, to a different realm altogether.
Man is unique, he is made in the image of God. So though the
animals are wonderful there was not one that could make a
companion for man, the companion that man needs. So we
go on, and read, 'And the Lord God caused a deep sleep to
fall upon Adam, and he slept; and he took one of his ribs and
closed up the flesh instead thereof; and the rib which the Lord
God had taken from man, made he a woman'. Woman is taken
out of man, out of his substance, out of 'his flesh', out of 'his
bones'. God takes a part out of man, and of that he makes
a woman. So what is woman? She is of the same substance
as man, 'of his flesh, and of his bones'. God performed the
operation. Man was put into a state of deep sleep, and then the

operation was performed, the part was taken out, and out of that woman was made.

'This is a great mystery; but I speak concerning Christ and the church'. 'We are members of his body, of his flesh, and of his bones'. How? Woman was made at the beginning as the result of an operation which God performed upon man. How does the church come into being? As the result of an operation which God performed upon the second man, his only begotten, beloved Son on Calvary's hill. A deep sleep fell upon Adam. A deep sleep fell upon the Son of God, he gave up the ghost, he expired, and there in that operation the church was taken out. As the woman was taken out of Adam, so the church is taken out of Christ. The woman was taken out of the side of Adam; and it is from the Lord's bleeding, wounded side that the church comes. That is her origin; and so she is 'flesh of his flesh, and bone of his bones'. 'This is a great mystery'.

Had you realized that? It is not an accident that the Lord Jesus Christ is referred to in the New Testament as the 'second man' or as the 'last Adam'. The apostle teaches here that this is true also of him in this respect. We normally think of our relationship to him in an individual sense, and that is right. Take the teaching concerning the relationship of the Christian to the Lord Jesus Christ as found in Romans chapter 5, where you have again this same comparison between the first man and the second man; it tells us how we are all involved in the transgression of Adam, and how we are involved in the righteousness of Christ. As the one, so the other. There the emphasis is upon the personal. Here, it is in terms of the church as a whole, the communal relationship; and this is the great mysterious truth which Paul is teaching. As it is true to say of the woman, that she was taken out of the side of man, out of the very substance, 'his flesh and his bones', so the church is taken out of Christ, and we are a part of him, members of his body and of his very bones. He is the last Adam, he is the second man. And as God operated on the first man to produce his bride, his help meet, so he has operated upon the second man to do the same thing in an infinitely more glorious manner.

But let us go on even further. We do so in fear and trembling; but let us go on. The apostle is emphasizing that we are a part of Christ's very nature. Note that he uses the word 'himself' in the twenty-eighth verse: 'No man', he says, 'ever yet hated his own flesh, but nourisheth and cherisheth it, even as the Lord the church. So ought men to love their wives as their own bodies. He that loveth his wife loveth himself'. Still the same idea! The body is a part of the man, and therefore when he pays attention to his body he is paying attention to himself. He cannot divorce himself from himself. What he does for his body he is doing for himself; he does it because it is a part of himself. That is the relationship between Christ and the church. That does not mean that we are divine. We must be careful about that. We Christians are not gods, nor are we divine. But what it does mean is that the Lord Jesus Christ is the former and beginner of a new humanity. One humanity started in Adam, a new humanity started in the Lord Jesus Christ. We are sharers of that! We are partakers of that! That is why we find Peter saying in his Second Epistle, chapter 1, verse 4, that we are 'partakers of the divine nature'. We are partakers of this nature that the mediator now has, having come through the incarnation and having done all that he came to do. We derive our life, our being from him, and we are truly parts of him.

But we must take the final step, and go to verses 31 and 32: 'For this cause shall a man leave his father and mother, and shall be joined unto his wife, and they two shall be one flesh. This is a great mystery, but I speak concerning Christ and the church'. Here, again, we can only understand the apostle's meaning by going back to the second chapter of Genesis. This verse is a direct quotation of Genesis 2:24. But what exactly does it mean? There are many who get frightened at this point and say: 'Ah, this is a great mystery and we must be careful that we do not press it too far'. So they say that the apostle introduced the words, 'they two shall be one flesh', the quotation from Genesis 2:24, simply to round off his quotation. But the apostle does not do that kind of thing; the apostle does not quote unless he has an object and a purpose in quoting. They say, 'Of course, this patently has nothing to do with the Lord Jesus Christ and the church. Here, Paul is really just talking about husbands and wives; he is not talking about the church at this point'. But I cannot accept that, for Paul says, 'This'—that which I have just been saying—'is a great mystery, but I speak concerning Christ and the church'.

I believe that this expression concerning the 'one flesh' applies to the relationship between Christ and the church as it does to the relationship between the husband and the wife. But let us be careful, because this is a great mystery. I am not attempting or pretending to say that I understand it fully, but at the same time I do not want to detract from the mystery. I want to get hold of this teaching concerning this mystical relationship, this extraordinary unity, this oneness that Paul is talking about. The following seems to me to be the explanation. Go back to Genesis 2 and this is what you find. Adam was originally one, a perfect, a complete man. And yet there was a kind of lack, there was no help meet for him. So what we are told is that God performed the operation, and this man who had been one now begins to be two—Adam and Eve, the man and the woman. The woman was taken out of him, so she is a part of him; she was not created from nothing as man was. She was taken out of the man, and so she is a part of man. But it did not stop there—and this is where I see the point of this mystery. In one sense they were now two, but in another sense they were not two: 'For this cause shall a man leave his father and mother and shall be joined to his wife, and they two shall become one flesh'. That is the very essence of the mystery.

There is a sense in which they are two, and there is a sense in which they are not two. We must never forget this unity, this oneness, this idea of the 'one flesh'.

Let us rise then to the topmost peak of the mystery. Adam was incomplete without Eve: and the deficiency, the lack, was made up by the creation of Eve. So there is a sense in which we can say that Eve makes up the 'fulness' of Adam, makes up that which was lacking in Adam. And that is exactly what the apostle says about the church in her relationship to Christ. Fortunately for us he has already said that in chapter 1, verse 23, which reads, 'which is his body'—he is talking about the church—'and gave him to be the head over all things to the church, which is his body, the fulness of him that filleth all in all'. The church is the 'fulness' of Christ. The church, he says, is that which 'makes up', as it were, this fulness of Christ. And I suggest that here in chapter 5 he is just repeating that truth. As Adam and Eve became one flesh, and as Eve makes up, as it were, the fulness of Adam, so the church makes up the fulness of Christ. That is the meaning attached to the word 'fulness' everywhere in the New Testament, as the authorites agree. Christ is not the fulness of the church, the church makes up his fulness, 'the fulness of him that filleth all in all'.

We can look at the matter in this way. The Lord Jesus Christ, as the eternal Son of God, is perfect, complete and entire, and always has been from all eternity—'in him dwelleth all the fulness of the Godhead bodily'. He is and always has been co-equal and co-eternal with the Father. The whole fulness of the Godhead is in each of the three persons. There is no lack, there is nothing to make up, there is no fulness which is lacking. But as the mediator, Christ is not full without the church. Now this is the mystery, the most glorious mystery of all. Jesus Christ as mediator will not be full and complete and entire until every soul has been gathered in for whom he died—'the fulness of the Gentiles' and 'all Israel'. It is only then that he will be full, only then will the fulness be complete.

This is the great mystery of salvation, and that is why we must be so careful. But the doctrine of salvation suggests this, that the blessed eternal Son of God, in order to save us, has put a limitation upon himself. In taking unto him human nature he took on a limitation. He remains God eternally—there is no limit on that, there is no lessening in his deity. It is a great mystery, and we must not try to understand it in an ultimate sense. It cannot be understood. But this is the teaching. There he is, one and unchangeable! Yes, but he became man, and he was subject to ignorance and infirmity when he was in this world, 'made in the likeness of sinful flesh'. And as the mediator, I say, he will not be complete until the church is entire. He has a bride to whom he is to be joined, and they become 'one flesh'. When the Lord Jesus Christ returned to heaven he did not leave his body behind, he took it with him. That human nature is in him now, and always will be. He is still the second person in the blessed Holy Trinity, but this human nature which you and I now have is there in him, and we shall be in him to all eternity. He has subjected himself to something. I venture on what is almost a speculation, but the apostle quotes these words: 'For this cause shall a man leave his father and mother and shall be joined unto his wife, and they two shall be one flesh'. I do not press the details but I say this—that the Lord Jesus Christ left the courts of glory and came into this world and on this earth for his bride. There has been a 'leaving' in his case, as in the case of a man who leaves his father and mother that he may be joined to his wife. Yes, he left the courts of glory—as Charles Wesley reminds us:

> He left His Father's throne above,
> So free, so infinite His grace!

He left heaven and the courts of glory for the sake of his bride. There was an awful moment when he cried out, 'My God, my God, why hast thou forsaken me?' For that moment he was separated from his Father. And why? Oh, that he might purchase and save this bride of his, who now, as the result of that operation, is a part of his body, of his flesh, and of his bones.

This is, I say, the supreme mystery. There is nothing more wonderful, there is nothing more glorious than this. We are sharers of his human nature, we are joined to him, and we shall be, throughout eternity. That is why we are told in the Scriptures that we shall be above the angels and 'judge' them. 'Know ye not', says Paul in 1 Corinthians 6, 'that the saints shall judge the world, that the saints shall judge angels?' Even angels! Why? Because we are raised above them; we are in the Son, we are a part of him, joined to him, 'one flesh' with him. The church is the bride of Christ, and as we think of this relationship we must always gaze into this mystery and realize that 'we are members of his body, of his flesh, and of his bones'. But above all let us realize what he did in order that we might become his. He left his Father's throne above, 'he humbled himself', 'he made himself of no reputation'—that is how he has loved the church! 'Husbands, love your wives, even as Christ also loved the church and gave himself for it.'

9. The Bride's Privileges

Ephesians 5:25-33

W E HAVE BEEN WORKING OUR WAY through this great statement which is primarily designed for the edification of
husbands, but which, as we have been seeing, has a glorious
message for all Christian people. This is so because the apostle in giving his message to the husband does so by using the
comparison of the relationship between Christ and the church.
That is the analogy that the husband is ever to bear in mind.

There is, however, one further thing for us to do before
we come to the application of the teaching to the particular
duties of husbands towards their wives. There is implicit in
what the apostle has been saying something further which
will be of great importance when we come to the practical
application, but which is also of inestimable value to us one
by one as Christian people as we realize our relationship to the
Lord Jesus Christ, and realize that together we are the bride of
Christ. Let me explain.

Because of all we have been considering it follows of necessity that the husband bestows certain things upon his bride;
and we are now going to look at what the Lord Jesus Christ
as the bridegroom of the bride, which is the church, bestows
upon her. As we do so we shall realize again the glorious privilege of being Christians and members of the Christian church.
I am holding you to this truth because it is my increasing and
profound conviction that the main problem, the main trouble, today is the failure of Christian people like ourselves to
realize the privilege, and the dignity, of being members of the

Christian church and of the body of Christ. I know, and I agree, that it is right to be concerned about the state of the world. We cannot be Christians without such a concern; but I cannot understand how anyone can be complacent about the state of the church. Surely the ultimate explanation of the state of the world is the state of the church. To me the saddest and the most grievous thing of all at the present time is the failure of Christian people to realize what the New Testament tells us about ourselves, and what it means to be members of the body of Christ. In a world that attaches such significance to honours and glories and position, is it not amazing that we can regard our membership of the church as we do? Many seem to regard it as almost a kind of dignity that they confer upon the church, instead of realizing that it is the highest and the most glorious privilege that anyone can ever have or know. Others regard their membership of the church as a task and as a duty, and are rather pleased with themselves if they perform any function. Now that betrays a complete failure to understand what it really means to be members of this body, which is the bride of the Lord Jesus Christ himself.

Let us therefore look at some of the things he bestows upon us, some of the things that are true of us as Christian people and members of the church. If the church but realized these things she would no longer be apologetic, and languishing, and drooping, and present such a miserable spectacle; she would be filled with a sense of pride and of joy and of glory.

What are the things he bestows upon us? The first is his life. We have already been looking at that truth, but I must mention it again in this connection. He gives us a part of his own life—we become sharers in his own life. That is what happens, is it not, when a man gets married? He was living his own life, but now he no longer lives his own life exclusively, his wife becomes a sharer in his life. As she is a part of him she is a sharer in his life and activity and everything that is true concerning him. The first thing a married man has to learn is that when he is confronted by various situations he now has to do something new. Before, the main problem for him was, How does this affect me, what is my reaction to this? But now he no longer stops at that. He now has to think also of how it will affect his wife. He no longer lives an isolated life, as it were, on his own; he has another to consider always who is a sharer of his life. Something may be acceptable to him, but there is somebody else to consider now.

I could elaborate on this; I could speak out of much pastoral experience of troubles and difficulties which I have had to deal with because husbands have forgotten just this very point. Let me give one illustration of it. I do so because it is one that I have often had to meet, and one concerning which I have often been misunderstood. But, taking that risk, I give it again in order to illustrate this point. A man has come to me and has said that he feels called to go to the foreign mission-field. Well, that is excellent. But then I have to ask a question—and I always do ask it if he is a married man—What does your wife say about it? Sometimes I have had to deal with men who do not seem to be concerned about that, and appear to regard the matter as if it were a purely personal decision. But it is not! A man has no right to isolate himself over a matter like that from his wife. Because the twain are one flesh, he has to consider his wife's views. We have already been dealing with the duties of wives towards their husbands. There is a great deal to be said on that side also; but the point I am establishing is that he is a very poor Christian who says, 'If I feel called to a particular work it does not matter what my wife says'. It does matter! That is a complete misunderstanding of this teaching.

But let us look at it from the other aspect, and realize that we are sharers of the life of the Lord Jesus Christ. It is a staggering thought, but we are entitled to say this, that we are ever in his mind; that in all his outlook we have our part and our place. We are 'in Christ', we are sharers of his life. The apostle in writing to the Colossians uses this extraordinary phrase in the third chapter and verse 4, 'When Christ, who is our life, shall appear'. He is 'our life', which is another way of saying that we are sharers of his life. Now there is nothing beyond that! We were really looking at that when studying the statement that 'we are members of his body, of his flesh, and of his bones'. We are now looking at it from a slightly different angle; not so much from the angle of the mystical union, but from that of the Lord's own consciousness that he is giving of his life, sharing it, and that we are taken into it, and become part and parcel of his life.

But let us go on to show this in its various manifestations. One is that he bestows upon us his name. We take on ourselves his name because he gives us his name. We are called 'Christians', and that is the greatest truth about us. We are no longer what we were, we have changed our names. A woman when she gets married changes her name. How important that becomes in helping us to understand the teaching of the great apostle in this fifth chapter of this Epistle to the Ephesians! What a lot it has to say also about this foolish modern movement called 'feminism'! When a woman gets married she gives up her name, she takes the name of her husband. That is biblical, and also the custom of the whole world. That teaches us the relationship between husband and wife. It is not the husband who changes his name, but the wife. There has been a striking illustration of this in recent times. I refer to it because I hope it will help to fix these truths in our mind. The whole nation knows what has happened in the case of Princess Margaret, how the name of her husband is always brought in when she is mentioned; and rightly so. It is unscriptural not to do so. It is the name of the husband that is taken, not the name of the wife. No matter who they are, this is the scriptural position.

But look at all this from our standpoint as members of the Christian church. Christ has put his name upon us. There is no greater compliment that can ever be paid us than that. That is the clearest expression of this married relationship. This is presented to us in many ways in the New Testament. 'There is no longer either Jew or Gentile, barbarian, Scythian, bond or free'. There used to be. Those were the names that we bore before. But no longer! We are now Christians, we have a new name. Or take the way in which this same apostle puts it in his Second Letter to the Corinthians, chapter 5: 'Henceforth', he says, 'know we no man after the flesh'. 'I used to know people after the flesh', he says; 'I as a Jew used to say, "What is that man, is he a Jew? If not, he is a mere dog". But', he says, 'I no longer think in those categories, I use new terms now. What I want to know is, "Is this man a Christian?" I do not care what his old name was; this is the name I am now interested in—"Christian!" Has he got the name of Christ on him?' So we realize that the Lord Jesus Christ bestows his name upon us. It is as real as this, says the apostle again, in writing to the Galatians, 'I live; yet not I, but Christ liveth in me'. That is the idea. Paul is submerged in a sense, yet he goes on to say: 'The life I now live in the flesh I live by the faith of the Son of God, who loved me, and gave himself for me'. What a wonderful statement that is of this married relationship! There is a sense in which the Christian's whole life is in the husband, and yet he has not become lost altogether, he is still there—'the life I now live in the flesh'.

There is the great mystery of the marriage relationship! But we must hold on to this great fact that the name of the Lord Jesus Christ is upon us. What matters, and should matter, to everyone of us is that we have changed our names. Here in the realm of the church the other names do not matter at all. It matters not what a man's name is, what his position or office is, what his ability is, what anything is. The one thing that

matters about him now is that the name of Christ is on him.
We are all one there, we are all together in him. He has taken
us to himself—the church is the bride of Christ. He says to us,
in effect,

> Forget that old name, take my name on you; you belong to me'.
> We find this in the Book of Revelation, chapter 3, verse 12: 'Him
> that overcometh will I make a pillar in the temple of my God, and
> he shall go no more out; and I will write upon him the name of my
> God, and the name of the city of my God, which is new Jerusalem,
> which cometh from heaven from my God: and I will write upon him
> my new name.

That is it!

> Write Thy new name upon my heart,
> Thy new best name of love.

This is the astounding thing that happens to all who are Christians, all who are members of this body, which is the bride
of Christ. You have been given a new name by the prince of
glory, and wonder of wonders! it is his own name. There is no
honour or glory greater than this. You are lost in a new name,
and it is the highest name of all. We read that a day is coming
when 'at the name of Jesus every knee shall bow, of things in
heaven, and things on earth, and things under the earth'—and
that is the name that is given to us who are constituted the
bride of Christ.

Then we see that out of that comes the fact that we are
sharers in his dignity, in his great and glorious position. The
apostle has already said as much in chapter 2 where he has
told us the amazing truth that 'he hath raised us up together [in
Christ], and made us sit together in heavenly places in Christ
Jesus'. That is true of us now. If we are Christians at all we are
'in Christ' and that means that we are 'seated with him in the
heavenly places'. Wherever the bridegroom is the bride is also,
and the standing, the dignity, and the position that belong to

him belong to her. It does not matter at all who she was; the moment she becomes his bride she shares all with him. And woe betide anyone who does not accord to her the position and the dignity! There is no greater insult that can be offered the bridegroom than a refusal to honour his bride. This is the truth, says the New Testament, about the Christian. It is something that we are told repeatedly. One statement of it occurs in the seventeenth chapter of John's Gospel, verse 22, where our Lord says: 'And the glory which thou gavest me I have given them'. The glory, he says, which the Father had given him he has given to his people. It is something that happens invariably in a marriage; the bride, being a part of the husband, and having his name on her, shares his whole position. 'The glory which thou gavest me I have given them.'

But take another statement of the matter. The Lord Jesus Christ said about himself, 'I am the light of the world'. That is his claim, and there is no higher claim. The world is in darkness, he says, apart from me. I am the only light that the world can ever receive, everything else is but an attempt of men to discover light; and they invariably fail. There is no light apart from Christ. But note what he says about us: 'Ye are the light of the world'. In other words, because he is what he is, and because of our relationship to him, we likewise become the light of the world. It is very difficult for us to realize it, is it not? We are but a small number in this pagan land of ours, only ten in a hundred claiming to be Christians, and only half of those attending the house of God. So we are apologetic, and somewhat ashamed of ourselves. But the truth about us is this: We are the light of the world! It is the Lord Jesus Christ who said that. This dark, evil world knows no light, and has no light, apart from the light which you and I are disseminating in it.

But think of the matter from the aspect of our dignity, our glory—what he is, he makes us. This is inevitable because of

the relationship. There are many other very wonderful statements of this. Listen to the Lord, again, in the Book of Revelation speaking to the church of the Laodiceans, of all people:
'To him that overcometh will I grant to sit with me in my
throne, even as I also overcame, and am set down with my
Father in his throne'. Because the church is the bride of Christ
she is going to sit with him in his throne. 'She is a commoner',
you say. Yes, but that does not matter; she is married to the
prince, and she shares the throne with him. That is the dignity,
that is the privilege he confers upon us!

Then attend to this. The Apostle Paul in trying to teach the
members of the church at Corinth something of this greatness
and glory puts it thus in chapter 6 of the First Epistle, verse 2:
'Do ye not know that the saints shall judge the world?' Then:
'Know ye not that we shall judge angels?' That refers to you
and me. Look at those miserable members of the church at Corinth. 'What is the matter with you?' asks the apostle. 'Why are
you quarrelling amongst yourselves? Why are you boasting of
this man or that man or another man, and taking one another
to the courts about disputes? Do you not realize that everyone
of you as a Christian is in such a relationship to Christ that you
are going to judge the world, that you are going to judge the
angels?' Here is the dignity that belongs to us.

Let me put it in this way. Think of the Christian in relationship to the angels. Had you realized that we are meant
for a destiny which will put us above the angels? The angels
are wonderful beings, they 'excel in strength'; but we are destined for a position which will be above that of the angels! The
author of the Epistle to the Hebrews puts it thus:

> For unto the angels hath he not put in subjection the world to come,
> whereof we speak. But one in a certain place testified, saying, What
> is man, that thou art mindful of him? or the son of man, that thou
> visitest him? Thou madest him a little lower than the angels; thou
> crownedst him with glory and honour, and didst set him over the

works of thy hands: Thou hast put all things in subjection under his feet (*Heb.* 2:5-8).

'But', says someone, 'I do not see all things put in subjection under man; what are you talking about?' 'O no', says the author of that epistle, 'we do not yet see all things put under him. But we see Jesus, who was made a little lower than the angels for the suffering of death, crowned with glory and honour' (verse 9). These words mean, that you and I are going to be in that position. We already have it in the sight of God; we do not see it, but it is true of us now. We are above the angels because we are the bride of Christ; and as he is above them in the heavenly places, we have that dignity and that greatness and that position even now.

That leads us to the next point, which is that we share not only in his life but in his privileges. The moment a woman becomes the bride of a man she shares his privileges. Whatever they are, she becomes partaker of them and sharer of them. The apostle is saying here that this is true of the church. What do we share? We share the Father's love. There is a verse which in many ways is to me the most astounding verse in the whole Bible. It is the twenty-third verse of the seventeenth chapter of John's Gospel. The Lord says, 'That the world may know that thou hast sent me, and hast loved them as thou hast loved me'. It is a statement to the effect that God the Father has loved us Christian people as he loves his own Son. What it means is that because of our relationship to him we are in that relationship to God. Think of a man, without daughters, whose son has got married. He now says to the bride of his son: 'You are my daughter. I never had a daughter before, but you are my daughter.' And he regards her as such. She is one with his son, therefore he bestows his fatherly love upon her—'that the world may know that thou hast loved them, as thou hast loved me'. That is the privilege. It works out in this way—it gives us access to the Father. A father is ever ready to receive the bride of his son. She did not have that access to him before; there was no relationship; but the moment she becomes married to the son she has a right of access into the presence of the father. As the father is ready to receive the son, and to give the son privileges which he would not grant to his most trusted and favourite servants, so now he grants them to the bride because she is the wife of his son. Christian people, do we avail ourselves of this high privilege? Do we realize that we have a right of entry and of access into the presence of the Father? Though he is the governor of the whole universe, if you have a need, remember that you have a right of entry to his presence. For his Son's sake he will not refuse you. Bride of Christ, he will always listen to you, he will always have time for you. There is no higher privilege than this. He loves us as he loves his Son, and he gives us this right of access and of entry into his holy presence.

Yet more, I am simply giving headings for you to think about and to meditate upon. We should spend much of our time with these points thinking about them. When you get on your knees to pray, do not start speaking immediately; stop and think. Think even before you get on your knees. Realize what you are doing; remember who you are, and because you are what you are, call to mind what is true of you, and the rights and privileges that are given you. Then go on to consider the possessions the Lord gives us. We are sharers in his possessions. The Apostle Paul in an extraordinary statement written to the church at Corinth says in effect: 'What are you troubling about? why are you divided amongst yourselves and jealous of one another, and envying one another? what is the matter with you? "All things are yours". Everything! I do not care what they are', says Paul, 'they are all yours. Why? "Because ye are Christ's, and Christ is God's".' Study that carefully in 1 Corinthians, at the end of chapter 4.

I ask again, Am I not right when I say that the real tragedy today is the failure of the church to realize the truth about herself? 'All things are yours'—everything! The cosmos is ours, in a sense, because we belong to Christ. The Apostle Paul was thrilled by this knowledge; and the test of our Christianity, the test of our spirituality, is as to whether we are moved and thrilled by these things. We may be having a hard time, we may be persecuted, we may be despised, people may be laughing at us because we are Christians. Do we know what we are to say to ourselves? We must say, 'Because we are children, we are therefore heirs; heirs of God and joint heirs with Christ' (*Rom.* 8:17). It matters little what the world may think or say—'All things are yours', Christians are 'joint heirs with Christ'.

But I particularly like the way in which this is expressed by the author of the Epistle to the Hebrews in the second chapter and verse 5. I have already quoted it, but I do so again: 'For unto the angels hath he not put in subjection the world to come, whereof we speak'. It is a pity that the Authorized Version translated it in that way. It is an awkward translation, it is an odd negative. 'For unto the angels hath he not put in subjection the world to come, of which we speak.' It means that 'he has not put the world to come, of which we speak, in subjection to angels, but to us'. What is this 'world to come' about which he is speaking? The 'world to come', of which he is speaking, is this old world in which you and I are living at this present time. Yes! but not as it is now. It is this same world when Christ shall have come back, and shall have destroyed all his enemies, and all evil, and every vestige and remains of evil; it is when the great burning shall have taken place, the great purification, the regeneration, when there shall be 'new heavens and a new earth wherein dwelleth righteousness'. That is the 'world to come' of which he is speaking. And this is a vital part of the essential Christian message. This world that we are in at this moment is only a passing world; this is not the real world, this is not the lasting world. What we see is the world as the result of what man has made it. We see the chaos that man has produced. The world itself, of course, is very interested in the visible and the present; and everybody is wondering what the latest conference is going to achieve—is there going to be disarmament, is war going to be banished, is everything going to be perfect for the rest of time? But that is all vain. This is an evil world, and evil and sin will go on manifesting themselves in it until God's appointed time of judgment shall arrive. But there is a 'world to come'; it is the new Jerusalem that will come down from heaven, this old world restored to all its pristine glory, this old world as God made it at the beginning, but yet more glorious. That will happen at Christ's second coming. He will dwell in it himself, and his bride with him. That is 'the world to come, of which we speak'. Who is going to live in that world, who is going to inherit that world? Well, says the epistle, it is not the angels: 'For not unto the angels hath he subjected the world to come, of which we speak', but unto us. We are the heirs of this glory that is to come. Christian people, do you ever envisage that? do you ever remind yourself of that? You may be having a hard time striving against the world, the flesh, and the devil; you may be facing difficulties and obstacles. Turn away from that! do not look at that alone! 'While we look not at the things which are seen, but at the things which are not seen; for the things which are seen are temporal, but the things which are not seen are eternal' (2 Cor. 4:18). Lift up your heads, you share Christ's inheritance, his possessions! You have married him—or rather, he has married you—and he puts these things into your hands. You are sharers of his possessions.

Let me again emphasize that we are sharers of his interests, his plans and his purposes. 'Co-workers together with God'. Do not think of your local church, or any other church in terms merely of yourself and what you are doing. The same applies to your denomination or movement. Rise above it, and consider his interests. I quote again, 'Ye are the light of the world'. The Lord has a purpose with respect to this world, and you and I are involved in, and sharers in that purpose. The husband tells his wife everything. She knows his every secret, his every desire, every ambition, every hope, every project that ever enters his mind. She is one with him. He tells her things that he would not say to anybody else; she shares everything, there is nothing kept back, nothing is hidden. Such is the relationship of husband and wife. It is also the relationship of Christ and the church; we are partners with him in this business of saving men. Do you know that interest? Do you feel it, do you think about it, do you prize the privilege of being sharers in the secret? Do you feel something of the burden, and are you helping him? That is what a Christian is for, that is what a wife is for—a help meet—and the church is the bride of Christ. How often do you pray for the success of the preaching of the gospel? To what extent are you concerned about the evangelistic message of the church? Do you think about it, do you feel you are a part of it, do you pray about it? A wife worthy of the name does not need to be exhorted to take an interest in her husband's affairs; she counts it her greatest privilege to be helping her husband; she is vitally interested in all he docs, and in its success. The church is the bride of Christ; he shares it all with us. Let us realize these things and rise to the dignity and privilege of it all.

But let me mention something which, to me, is one of the most fascinating and charming aspects of it all. The Lord not only shares his possessions, his interests, his plans and his purposes with us; he shares his servants with us. You may have been a Cinderella, the whole church was a Cinderella, in her rags, slaving and having a hard and a difficult life, doing all the chores for the other sisters. But Cinderella is married to the prince; and what happens? Instead of having to slave in that way she now has her servants. Whose servants? His servants! Because she has become the bride of this prince all his servants are her servants, and they minister to her as they do to him. Had you realized that this is true of us? Let us go back once more to the Epistle to the Hebrews, and to the first chapter. The writer is comparing and contrasting the Lord Jesus Christ with the angels, and this is how he expresses it: 'Unto which of the angels said he at any times, Sit on my right hand, until I make thine enemies thy footstool'. Then: 'Are they not all ministering spirits, sent forth to minister for them who shall be heirs of salvation?'

What it means is that because we are Christians the angels of God are our servants. That is how the epistle describes an angel. An angel is a 'ministering spirit', who is sent forth to serve and to minister to us who are the heirs of the 'world to come' of which he is speaking. I fear that we neglect the ministry of angels; we do not think sufficiently about it. But whether we realize it or not, there are angels who are looking after us; they are round and about us. We do not see them, but that does not matter. We do not see the most important things; we only see the things that are visible. But we are surrounded by angels; and they are appointed to look after us and to minister to us—guardian angels. I do not pretend to understand it all; I know no more than the Bible tells me—but I do know this, that his servants, the angels, are my servants. They are surrounding us all, they are looking after us, and they are manipulating things for us in a way we cannot understand. And I further know that when we come to die they will carry us to our appointed place. It is the Lord Jesus himself who taught that fact in the parable of Dives and Lazarus in Luke 16. We are told that the rich man died and was buried. But what happened to Lazarus? He was 'carried by the angels into Abraham's bosom'. Do we realize that the angels of God are ministering unto us because we are the bride of the Son? From their origin they have ministered to him, and they have waited upon him; and because of the new relationship they are now our servants, ministering to us. May God give us grace to realize that we are surrounded by such ministries, and ministrations, and by such ministers! Nothing can finally harm us; they are there, sent by him to look after us.

But remember that we are also sharers of his problems and of his troubles and of his sufferings. He said, 'If they have persecuted me, they will also persecute you'. He spoke of hatred also. Do we share something of his problems? are we aware of this? 'My little children', says Paul to the Galatians, 'of whom I travail in birth again until Christ be formed in you'. He felt something of the pain. But he says in a still more striking manner in Colossians 1:24: 'Who now rejoice in my sufferings for you, and fill up that which is behind of the afflictions of Christ in my flesh for his body's sake, which is the church'. The Apostle Paul was so conscious of this relationship to the Lord Jesus Christ that he said that he was filling up in his own body something that remained of the 'sufferings of Christ'. A wife worthy of the name suffers whenever her husband suffers; she suffers in her heart as she sees him suffering; she shares it with him, she bears it with him. So did the Apostle Paul make up in his own body something of what remained of the sufferings of Christ as he works out his purpose in the world, the agony of the Son of God, that will continue until the 'crowning day' arrives. The church is the bride of Christ. Do we as parts and portions of the body know something of this agony, this suffering, the sufferings of the head?

Finally, we share in all the glory of his prospects. I refer to 'the world to come' once more. 'When Christ, who is our life, shall appear, then shall we appear with him in glory' (*Col.* 3:4). 'A glorious church, not having spot, or wrinkle, or any such thing; but that she might be holy and without blemish'— when he comes in his glory. If we shall have already died, we shall come with him; if we are still alive, we shall be changed and caught up to meet him in the air. We shall share in everlasting glory with the Son of God. This is his special prayer to the Father (*John* 17:24): 'Father, I will that they also whom thou hast given me, be with me where I am, that they may behold my glory, which thou hast given me'. 'The glory which thou gavest me, I have given them.' We shall share it with him through all eternity. Is there anything that is comparable to this, to being members of the body of Christ, to being, as parts of the church, the bride of Christ?

Shame on us for our weakness, our helplessness, our complaining, our lethargy, our half-envying the world and the so-called wonderful life it has, its joy and enjoyment so-called. It is a dying world; it is an evil world; it is under condemnation; and it is going to disappear. It is already 'passing away'. But you and I have this glory to look forward to, the glory that we shall share with the Lord Jesus Christ in that great day. The glory of that 'world to come' is indescribable; and we shall live and reign with him in it.

Having taken the church as his bride, he bestows all that upon her. His prospects are ours, his glory is ours, all things are ours. 'The meek shall inherit the earth.' We shall reign with him over the whole universe, we shall judge angels. You and I! Such is the Christian! Such is the Christian church as the bride of Christ!

10. The Husband's Duties

Ephesians 5:25-33

IN CONSIDERING THIS STATEMENT we have seen that there are two main themes. One is the theme of the relationship between the Lord Jesus Christ and the church, and the other is the relationship between the husband and the wife. The apostle's teaching is that we can only truly understand the relationship of husband and wife as we understand the great doctrine of Christ and the church. We have therefore been considering the doctrine of Christ and the church first, and having done so we are now in a position to begin the application of that, particularly to the husbands, though, as you notice, the apostle is careful at the end (verse 33) to consider it also from the aspect and the standpoint of the wife. The application of the doctrine is introduced by the terms 'even as' and 'so'. 'Husbands, love your wives even as'—and then at the end, 'Nevertheless let everyone of you in particular so love his wife even as himself.' In other words, he is working out the comparison, which he has unfolded before us, of the relationship of Christ to the church in terms of the relationship of the husband to the wife.

As we come, then, to the application it seems to me that the best way of handling it is to divide it into two main sections. The first is that in which certain principles are taught with respect to husbands and their wives. Then, having laid down the general principles, we can move on to the second, which is the detailed practical application of the principles to the concrete situation.

The general principles, as I see them, are these. First, we must realize in connection with marriage, as indeed with everything else in the Christian life, that the secret of success is to think and to understand. That is surely obvious, on the very surface of the passage. Nothing happens automatically in the Christian life. That is a very profound principle, for I believe that most of our troubles arise from the fact that we tend to assume that they do happen automatically. We persist in holding on to a semi-magical notion of regeneration which teaches that, because of what has happened to us, the rest of the story is, quite simply, 'they all lived happily ever after'. But of course we know that that is not true. There are problems in the Christian life; and it is because so many do not realize that it is not something that works automatically, that they get into trouble and into difficulties. Obviously the antidote to that is to think, to have an understanding, to reason the thing out thoroughly. The world does not do that. The trouble with the world, ultimately, according to the teaching of the Bible, is that it does not think. If only people thought, most of their problems would be solved.

Take the problem of war for instance. War is something which is inherently ridiculous; it is insane. Why then do people fight? The answer is, because they do not think. They act instinctively, they are governed by primitive instincts such as desire and greed, anger, and so on; and they hit before they think. If only they all stopped to think, there would be no more war. The fallacy of the humanist is, of course, that he believes that all you have to do therefore is to tell people to think. But as long as they are sinners they will not think. These elemental forces are so much stronger than the rational forces that 'man in sin' is always irrational.

When we become Christians we still need to enforce this self-same principle. Even the Christian does not think automatically; he has to be taught to think — hence these New Testament epistles. Why were they ever written? If a man who becomes a Christian automatically does the right thing, why did the

apostle ever have to write these epistles? Or if you can receive
your sanctification as one act, one blessing, why were these
epistles ever written? Here they are, full of reason, full of argument, full of demonstrations, full of analogies and comparisons.
Why? In order to teach us how to think, in order to teach us
how to work these things out, and how to gain understanding.

Thinking is essential, as the apostle shows, in connection
with this whole subject of marriage. The world views marriage
in the following way. It more or less first of all takes certain
great things for granted. It relies upon what it calls 'love', it
relies upon feelings. Two people say that they have 'fallen in
love' with each another, and on the strength of that they get
married. They do not stop to think and to ask questions; to do
so is very exceptional. They are moved and animated and carried away by the feeling that everything is bound to go well,
that their happiness is certain to last and can never fail. All this
is encouraged by the popular literature and by the films shown
in cinemas and in the home on the television set. But then you
read the newspapers and their reports and you find that it does
fail. Why does it fail? The answer is, because they have never
thought the matter through; and therefore it cannot stand up
to the tests and the stresses and the strains that must inevitably
come as life is lived from day to day with its weary round and
its physical tiredness and the many other things that produce
difficulties. And it is because such people have never thought
the thing through that they have nothing to fall back upon.
They have acted on a feeling, on an impulse; they have acted
emotionally. The mind has scarcely come in at all, with the
result that when they are confronted by difficulties they have
no arguments to fall back upon. They do not know what to
do; everything seems to have gone; and so they panic and sue
for a divorce immediately; and many repeat the same process
time and again. The whole cause of the trouble is an absence
of understanding, a lack of thought.

When you consider the Christian position you find the main difference to be this—that the Christian is exhorted to think and to understand, and is given a basis on which he can do so. That is the meaning and purpose of this teaching which is provided for us; so we are left without excuse if we neglect it. The world has no such teaching, but we are no longer in that position. So the first thing we are reminded of by this paragraph is that we must think. We are even told how to do so, and it is put before us in detail. That is the first principle.

The second principle is that as Christians our conception of marriage must be positive. The danger is that we should think of marriage amongst Christians as essentially the same as it is with everybody else, the only difference being that these two people happen to be Christians whereas the others are not. Now if that is still our conception of marriage then we have considered this great paragraph entirely in vain. Christian marriage, the Christian view of marriage, is something that is essentially different from all other views. That is, surely, what has been emerging as we have worked our way through this paragraph.

Here we get a view of marriage which is not possible but within the Christian faith; it is lifted up to the position of the relationship between the Lord Jesus Christ and the church. So the Christian's attitude towards marriage is always a positive one, and he should always be straining after this ideal. The Christian's view must not be negative in the sense that, because certain new factors have entered in, therefore this marriage ought to last, whereas the other one is not likely to do so. That is purely negative. It is not merely that we avoid certain things that are true of the others; we must have this ideal, positive conception of marriage. It is something that we must always think of in terms of the relationship of the Lord Jesus Christ and the church. We have to learn to test ourselves constantly by asking the question: Does my married life really correspond

to that relationship? Is it manifesting it? Is it being governed
by it ? In other words, in the Christian position we do not stop
thinking about these things when we have been married a few
months. We go on thinking, and we think more and more, and
the more Christian we become and the more we grow in grace,
the more we think about our marriage, and the more we are
concerned that it should conform to this heavenly pattern, to
this glorious ideal of the relationship between the Lord Jesus
Christ and the church. This is something which it is difficult to
put into words. What I am trying to convey is that the great
difference between the marriage of Christians and the marriage
of non-Christians should be that in the case of the Christians
the marriage becomes progressively more wonderful, more
glorious, as it conforms to, and attains to the ideal increasingly. We all, surely, see the significance of that as we apply
it to what is so commonly true of marriage, not only among
non-Christians but, alas, among Christians also. The Christian
conception of marriage is one which continues to grow and
develop and increase.

My third and last general principle is one that has come out
in the whole of the exposition—that the real cause of failure,
ultimately, in marriage is always self, and the various manifestations of self. Of course that is the cause of trouble everywhere
and in every realm. Self and selfishness are the greatest disrupt-
ing forces in the world. All the major problems confronting
the world, whether you look at the matter from the standpoint
of nations and statesmen, or from the standpoint of industry
and social conditions, or from any other standpoint—all these
troubles ultimately come back to self, to 'my rights', to 'what I
want', and to 'who is he?' or 'who is she?' Self, with its horrid
manifestations, always leads to trouble, because if two 'selfs'
come into opposition there is bound to be a clash. Self always
wants everything for itself. That is true of my self, but it is
equally true of your self. You at once have two autonomous

powers, each deriving from self, and a clash is inevitable. Such clashes occur at every level, from two people right up to great communities and empires and nations.

The apostle's teaching in the verses under consideration is designed to show us how to avoid the calamities that result from self. That is why I was at such pains to emphasize verse 21 before we began to consider the question of marriage. It is the key to the entire paragraph—'Submitting yourselves one to another in the fear of God'. That is the basic principle, and it is to be true of all members of the Christian church. Whether married or unmarried, we are all to be submitting ourselves one to the other in the fear of God. Then the apostle goes on to apply the principle to the particular case of man and woman, husband and wife, and he has made it so plain and clear that surely no-one can miss it. What is the essential thing about marriage? He says, it is this unity—these two, these twain, have become one flesh. So you must stop thinking of them as two, they have become one. Therefore any tendency to assert self at once conflicts with the fundamental conception of marriage. In marriage, says the apostle, it should be unthinkable for such a conflict to arise, for to think of these two as two is to deny the basic principle of marriage, which is that they are one. 'These two shall be one flesh'. The wife is 'the body' of the husband, even as the church is the body of Christ—and so on. So here we have, above everywhere else, the final denunciation of self and all its horrid manifestations; and we are shown the one and only way whereby we can finally be delivered from it.

Those are the three general principles which, in marriage, underlie the practical application of the doctrine of the relationship of the Lord Jesus Christ to the church. Now the husband is to be governed by these principles. How does this work out in practice? First of all, the husband must realize that his wife is a part of himself. He will not feel this instinctively; he has to be taught it; and the Bible in all its parts teaches it. In other words, the husband must understand that he and his wife are not two: they are one. The apostle keeps on repeating that: 'So ought men to love their wives as their own bodies'. 'He that loveth his wife loveth himself'; 'they two shall be one flesh'. 'We are members of his body, of his flesh, and of his bones'. That is all true of our relationship to the Lord, it is true also in this other relationship.

I would therefore put it in this way, that it is not sufficient for us even to regard our wives as partners. They are partners, but they are more than partners. You can have two men in business who are partners, but that is not the analogy. The analogy goes higher than that. It is not a question of partnership, though it includes that idea. There is another phrase that is often used—at least, it used to be common—which puts it so much better, and which seems to me to be an unconscious statement of the Christian teaching. It is the expression used by men when they refer to their wives as 'my better half'. Now that is exactly right. She is not a partner, she is the other half of the man. 'They two shall be one flesh'. 'My better half'. The very word 'half' puts the whole case which the apostle elaborates here. We are not dealing with two units, two entities, but dealing with two halves of one—'They two shall be one flesh'. Therefore, in the light of this, the husband must no longer think singly or individually. That should be quite impossible in marriage, says the apostle, because, 'He that loveth his wife loveth himself'. He is in a sense not loving somebody else, he is loving himself. Such is the difference that marriage makes.

On the practical level, therefore, the whole of the husband's thinking must include his wife also. He must never think of himself in isolation or in detachment. The moment he does so he has broken the most fundamental principle of marriage. Everybody sees it when it happens on the physical level, but the real damage is done before that, on the intellectual and the spiritual level. In a sense, the moment a man thinks of himself in isolation he has broken the marriage. And he has no right to do that! There is a sense in which he cannot do it, because the wife is a part of himself. But if it happens he is certain to inflict grievous damage on his wife; and it is a damage in which he himself will be involved because she is a part of him. He is therefore even acting against himself, did he but realize it. His thinking, therefore, must never be personal in the sense of being individualistic. He is only the half, and what he does involves of necessity the other half. The same applies to his desires. He must never have any desire for himself alone. He is no longer one man, he is no longer free in that sense; his wife is involved in all his desires. It is his business therefore to see that he is always fully alive to these considerations. He must never think of his wife, in other words, as an addition. Still less—I am sorry that I have to use such an expression—as an encumbrance; but there are many who do so.

To sum it up, this is a great commandment to married men never to be selfish. Neither must the wife be selfish, of course. Everything applies on the other side, but here we are dealing particularly with husbands. We have already seen that the wife is to submit herself. In doing so she has acted on the same principle; this is now the husband's side of the matter. He must therefore deliberately remind himself constantly of what is true of him in this married state, and that must govern and control all his thinking, all his wishing, all his desiring, indeed the totality of his life and activity.

But we can go further and put this more strongly. Verse 28 closes with the words, 'He that loveth his wife loveth himself'; but we remember that the apostle, in describing the relationship between the Lord and the church, has used the analogy of the body. 'So', he further says, in the same verse, 'So ought men to love their wives as their own bodies'. Then he elaborates it in verse 29: 'For no man ever yet hated his own flesh; but nourisheth and cherisheth it, even as the Lord the church'.

Here, then, is the teaching—that we not only have to realize that the husband and wife are one, but the husband must realize that the wife is actually a part of himself according to this analogy of the body. A man's attitude to his wife, says the apostle, should be his attitude, as it were, to his body. That is the analogy—and it is more than an analogy. We have already considered the matter as it is taught at the end of Genesis chapter 2. The woman was originally taken out of the man. There we have the proof of the fact that she is a part of the man, and that describes the characteristic of the unity. The man therefore is told this: 'So ought men to love their wives as their own body'. Now that little word 'as' is a most important and vital one, because we can easily misunderstand it. Paul does not say, 'So ought men to love their wives in the same way as they love their bodies'. That is not the meaning. The meaning is, 'So ought men to love their wives because they are their own bodies'. A man loves his wife as his body—that is what he is saying. Not 'as' he loves his body so must he love his wife. No! a man must love his wife as his body, as a part of himself. As Eve was a part of Adam, taken out of his side, so the wife is to the man, because she is a part of him.

I am stressing this for the reason which the apostle brings out clearly, namely, to show that there is this element of indissolubility about marriage, which, as I understand the biblical teaching, can only be broken by adultery. But what we are concerned to say now, is that the apostle puts it in this form in order that a husband may see that he cannot detach himself from his wife. You cannot detach yourself from your body, so you cannot detach yourself from your wife. She is a part of you, says the apostle, so remember that always. You cannot live in isolation, you cannot live in detachment. If you realize that, there will be no danger of your thinking in detachment, no danger of your wishing and willing and desiring any detachment. Still less can there be any antagonism or hatred.

Notice how he puts it: 'No man', he says, to ridicule the thing, 'no man ever yet hated his own flesh but nourisheth and cherisheth it, even as the Lord the church'. So any element of hatred between husband and wife is sheer madness; it shows that the man has no conception at all as to what marriage means. 'No man hated his own flesh'—but his wife is his own flesh, she is his body; so he is to love his wife as his own body.

What does this lead to in practice? Here I come to very detailed teaching which is needed by all, Christian people as well as others. God knows, we all have failed; we all have sinned by failing to understand this teaching and to apply it in detail. The principle is that the wife is, as it were, the body of the man. So what his body is to his personality his wife should be to him. Out of that comes the apostle's detailed teaching. How is a man to treat his wife? Let me give some negatives first. He is not to abuse her. It is possible for a man to abuse his body, and many men do abuse their bodies—by eating too much, by drinking too much, and in various other ways. That is to abuse the body, to maltreat it, to be unkind to it. Now, says the apostle, a man who does that is a fool, because if a man maltreats his body, and abuses it, he himself is going to suffer. You cannot detach yourself from your body; and if you think you can, and abuse your body, you will be the one to suffer. Your mind will suffer, your heart will suffer, the whole of your life will suffer. You may say, 'I do not care about my body, I am living a life of the intellect'; but if you keep on doing that you will soon find that you no longer have the intellect that you once had, and you will not be able to think as you once did. If you abuse your body, you are the one who is going to suffer. Not only the body, but you yourself will suffer as well. It is exactly the same in the married relationship. If a man abuses his wife he will suffer as well as the wife. So, apart from the inherent wrongfulness, the man is a fool. If a man abuses his wife there is going to be a breakdown not only in the wife but also in the man, and in the relationship between the two. Surely this is what is happening so commonly in the world today. It should be unthinkable that a Christian man should abuse his wife.

But not only should the husband not abuse his wife, in the second place, he should not neglect her. Come back again to the analogy of the body. A man can neglect his body. It often happens, and again it always leads to trouble. To neglect the body is bad, it is foolish, it is wrong. Man has been so constituted that he is body, mind and spirit, and the three are in intimate relationship one with another. We are all surely aware of this. Take an example in terms of the frailty of the body. If I am suffering from laryngitis I cannot preach, though I may want to do so. I may be full of ideas, and of a desire to preach, but if my throat is inflamed I cannot speak. And it is so with the whole of the body. If you neglect the body you yourself will suffer for it. Many a man has done that, many a scholar has done that, and through neglect of the body his work has suffered. That is because of the essential unity between these parts of our personalities.

It is exactly the same in the married relationship, says the apostle. How much trouble is caused in the realm of marriage simply because of neglect! Very recently there has been evidence in the papers by medical men who have reported that large numbers of wives today have been driven to chain smoking. Why? Simply because they have been neglected by their husbands. The husbands spend their nights out at sports, or in their public house, or playing games with their friends; and the poor wife is left at home with the children and the work. The husband comes home at night just in time to go to bed and to sleep; and he gets up and goes out in the morning. Neglect of the wife is leading to these nervous conditions that reveal themselves in excessive smoking and other manifestations of nervous tension. It is lamentable that a man should get married and then proceed to neglect his wife. In other words, here is a man who has married, but who in essential matters goes on living as if he were still a bachelor. He is still living his own detached life, he still spends his time with his men friends.

I could elaborate on this very easily, but the facts are so familiar that it is unnecessary. But I have a feeling that I detect a tendency even in Christian circles, and even in evangelical circles, to forget this particular point. A married man must no longer act as if he were a single man; his wife should be involved in everything. I recently received an invitation to a social occasion in connection with some evangelical organization; but the invitation was addressed to me only, and not to my wife also. I automatically refused it, as I always do when that kind of thing happens. This was an instance of an evangelical organization that is obviously not thinking clearly about these matters. I venture to lay it down as a rule that a Christian man should not accept an invitation to a social occasion without his wife. There is irreparable damage done to many marriages because men meet alone in their clubs without their wives. That is wrong, because it is a denial of first principles. Man and wife should do things together. Of course, the man in his business has to be alone, and there are other occasions when he has to be alone; but if it is a social occasion, something into which a wife can enter, she should enter, and it is the business of the husband to see to it that she does enter. I suggest that all Christian husbands should automatically refuse every such invitation which comes to them alone and does not include their wives.

But there is another aspect of this matter that at times causes me great concern. I am constantly hearing of what sometimes has been called 'evangelical widows'. The expression means that the husband of that particular type of woman is a man who is out every night at some meeting or other. His explanation, indeed his argument, is that he is engaged in good Christian work; but he seems to forget that he is a married man. At the other extreme, of course, there is the kind of Christian who does nothing, but who just indulges himself and his laziness, and spends all his time at home. Both extremes are wrong always; but at the moment I am condemning this particular extreme — the case of the man who is so busy with Christian work that he neglects his wife. I have known many cases of this. I was told of one recently in the north of England — the case of a man who was out speaking at meetings, organizing this and that, every night. The man who told me confessed that he had been tending to do the same thing himself, but that suddenly he had been awakened when he had met the wife of this other man about whom everybody was talking. He said that the poor little woman appeared like a slave; she looked exhausted, weary, tired, neglected and unhappy, and sick at heart. The conduct of such a husband is grievously sinful. Though it is done in the name of active Christian work, a man cannot and must not contract out of his married relationship in that way, because the wife is a part of him — his 'better half', not his slave. Christian husbands must therefore examine themselves in this matter. A home is not a dormitory where a man returns to sleep. No! there is to be this active, ideal, positive relationship; and we must ever be holding it in the forefront of our mind. A man therefore must seek wisdom from God to know how to divide himself up in this respect. But I care not what a man is; if he is a married man, he must not behave as a single man, even in connection with Christian work, because in so doing he is denying the very teaching of the gospel which he claims to be preaching. There can be untold selfishness just at that point. This generally happens, I know, as the result of nothing worse than thoughtlessness; but thoughtlessness generally leads to selfishness. In any case a Christian should not be guilty of thoughtlessness.

So I move on to the third practical outworking of the teaching. The husband must not abuse his wife, he must not neglect his wife, and, thirdly, he must never take her for granted. The positive element must always be there. A man's wife is not just his housekeeper; there is this positive element. How can that best be brought out? Let me take the apostle's own terms. He puts it like this: 'So ought men to love their wives as their own bodies. He that loveth his wife loveth himself. No man ever yet hated his own flesh; but' — What? — 'nourisheth and cherisheth it even as the Lord the church'. You remember how, when we considered these words, we were amazed and staggered at the way in which the Lord nourishes and cherishes us. But that is the way in which a husband should behave towards his wife. 'Nourisheth and cherisheth'. Again, you cannot do this without thinking.

Once more, this can be worked out in terms of the analogy that a man does not hate his own body, but nourishes it and cherishes it. How does he do so? We can divide it up simply thus: First of all, there is the question of diet. A man has to think about his diet, about his food. He has to take sufficient nourishment, he has to take it regularly, and so on. All that must be worked out in terms of husband and wife. The man should be thinking of what will help his wife, what will strengthen his wife. As we take our food we not only think in terms of calories, or protein, fat, and carbohydrate; we are not purely scientific, are we? Another element comes into this question of food. We are influenced also by what appeals to the palate, by what gives us pleasure and enjoyment. So ought the husband to treat his wife. He should be thinking of what pleases her, what gives her pleasure, what she likes, what she enjoys. Of course, before he got married he went out of his way to do this; but then after he gets married he often stops doing so. Is not that the difficulty? Very well, says the apostle, you must not stop, you must go on thinking; and as you are a Christian, you should engage in thinking more and more, not less and less. That is his argument. Are we not all condemned? But this is the apostolic teaching, the New Testament teaching. Diet—consider her whole personality and her soul. There has to be this active thought about the development of the wife, and her life, in this amazing relationship which God himself has established.

Again, there is the question of exercise. The analogy of the body suggests that at once. Exercise for the body is essential; exercise is equally essential in the married relationship. It can mean as simple a thing as this—just talking. Alas, I have known trouble in marriages so often, simply because of an absence of conversation. We all know how much there is to be said by way of excuse. A man is tired, he has been at his work or his office all day, and he comes home weary and tired, and wants rest and peace. Yes, but the same thing is also true of his wife, with the difference that perhaps she has been alone all day, or only had the society of little children. Whether we feel like it or not we must talk. The wife needs exercise in this sense. Tell her about your business, about your worries, about your affairs; bring her into it. She is your body, she is a part of you, so allow her to speak concerning it. Consult her, let her bring her understanding to bear. She is a part of your life, so bring her into the whole of your life. Make yourself talk. In other words, one has to force oneself to think. I repeat once more that I know all the excuses, and how difficult it often can be; but let me put it like this—I think it is a fair argument. This man was equally tired and working equally hard before he got married; but in the days before marriage, whatever he had been doing, he was most anxious to talk to his fiancée and to bring her into everything. Why should that stop when they get married? It should not stop, says the apostle. The husband and wife are one. Look at her, and consider her as you do your body, and remember this element of exercise. Bring her into everything deliberately. It will be wonderful for her, for her development; and it will be good for you yourself, because the whole marriage will grow and develop as you do so.

And that brings us to the fourth point, which is the element of protection. Here is this body, it needs food, it needs exercise; but in addition every man has to learn to understand his own body. The apostle works out the argument. The Apostle Peter, you remember, puts it like this. He tells the husband to remember that his wife is 'the weaker vessel'. This means that these bodies of ours are subject to certain things. We are all different even in a physical sense. Some of us are subject, perhaps, to feeling the cold, or subject to chills in a way that does not seem to worry other men. Some of us are so constituted that we have these minor problems; and we are subject to odd infections and various other things that come to try us. What does a wise man do? He takes great care about such things; he puts on a heavy overcoat in winter, he may put on a scarf; and he refrains from doing certain things. He is protecting himself and his weak constitution against some of the hazards that come to meet us in life. 'So ought men to love their wives'. Have you discovered that your wife has some peculiar temperamental weakness? Have you discovered that she has certain special characteristics? Is she nervous and apprehensive; or is she too outspoken? It does not matter what it is in particular; she has certain characteristics which are, in a sense, weaknesses. What is your reaction to them? Are you irritated, or annoyed? And do you tend to condemn them and to dismiss them? Act as you do with your body, says the apostle. Protect her against them, guard her against them. If your wife happens to have been born with that worrying temperament, well, save her from it, protect her. Do everything you can to safeguard her from the weaknesses and the infirmities and the frailties; as you do so for your body, do so for your wife.

Then, of course, there are great infections that come—a wave of influenza, fevers, things that kill people by the thousand. Corresponding things come also in the married life—trials, troubles, tribulations, which are going to test the marriage to the very limit.

What do we do about these? Once more, what do you do with your body when you get that kind of illness, when you get that attack of influenza with a raging temperature? The answer is that you put yourself to bed, with a hot-water bottle; and you put yourself on the appropriate diet, and so on. You do everything you can to treat the fever and to help your body to resist it. 'So ought men to love their wives as their own bodies'. If there is some peculiar, exceptional trial or anxiety or problem, something that tests your wife to the uttermost, then, I say, the husband is to go out of his way to protect his wife and to help her and aid her. She is 'the weaker vessel'.

That brings us to the last point. You try to protect your body against infections by having various inoculations. Apply all that to the married state. Do everything you can to build up the resistance, to prepare your wife to face the hazards of life. You have to build her up. Do not do everything yourself, as it were; but build her up so that she will be able to act also; so that if you are taken away by death she is not left stranded. We have to think out all these things in detail exactly as with the care of the body. And if an illness comes, take extra care, give the appropriate medicaments, go out of your way to do those extra things which will promote and produce the restoration of health and vigour and happiness.

We leave it at that. But, there, we have been looking at one big principle which is most important. A man has to love his wife 'even as'—because she is—his own body. 'No man ever yet hated his own flesh; but nourisheth and cherisheth it, even as the Lord the church'. 'Husbands, love your wives, even as Christ also loved the church'.

11. Transformed Relationships

Ephesians 5:25-33

WE COME TO OUR FINAL CONSIDERATION of this most important and extraordinary statement. The apostle is dealing primarily with the duty of husbands towards their wives, though in the last verse, you notice, he again reverts to the duty of wives towards their husbands, in order that he may present his teaching concerning marriage as a whole and in a complete form. In applying all this we have seen that the great thing is to understand the teaching. The Christian, of all people, should be one who thinks and reasons, who employs his mind. There is nothing magical about the Christian life. The great act of regeneration is the operation of God, but the moment we receive life we are able to think and to reason and to use our understanding. So all these New Testament epistles are addressed to the understanding. At the beginning of this very epistle the apostle has prayed 'that the eyes of your understanding might be enlightened' by the Holy Spirit. So we have found that what the apostle does here is to set out this great doctrine of Christ and the church and then say, 'Even so, just like that'.

There are a few practical points which must be dealt with in order that our exposition may be complete. There are certain practical injunctions which the apostle gives here, and they are all related to this great analogy which he uses. The great vital principle is that unity. What we have to grasp is the essential unity between the husband and wife—'these two shall be made [or become] one flesh'. This unity is comparable to the unity between a man and his own body, and also to the mystical union between Christ and the church.

Unity is the central principle in marriage; and it is because so many people in this modern world have never had any conception of what is involved in marriage, from the standpoint of unity, that they are riding so loosely to it and breaking their vows and pledges, so much so that divorce has become one of the major problems of our age. They have never caught sight of this unity; they still think in terms of their individuality, and so you have two people asserting their rights, and therefore you get clashes and discord and separation. The answer to all that, says Paul, is to understand this great principle of unity.

The apostle has worked that out in terms of the body, but now he puts it very explicitly by reminding us again of what is said in the second chapter of Genesis in connection with the making of Eve out of Adam, that Adam might have an 'help meet'. The moment God made Eve, in order that the man and the woman might enter into this married state, the statement was made that a man should leave his father and mother and should be joined unto his wife, and 'they shall be one flesh'. The apostle quotes the very words in verse 21: 'For this cause shall a man leave his father and mother, and shall be joined unto his wife, and they two shall be one flesh'. This is a command which is given to the man who is becoming a husband. He has to leave his father and mother. Why has he to do so? Because of this new unity that is coming into being between him and his wife. 'For this cause', says the apostle. What is that cause? He has just told us—'We are members of his body, of his flesh, and of his bones'. That is the relationship of husband and wife, and because of that—'for this cause'—a man must leave his father and mother in order that he may thus be joined to his wife.

This is a most important point. It is, in a way, the final proof of the unity that exists in true marriage, and it is an external indication of the unity. The apostle is saying, in other words, that when a man gets married he enters into a new unity that breaks former relationships. He is no longer to be bound and held by the former relationships because he is entering into a new and into a more intimate relationship of unity. Until he got married the man's chief loyalty was to his father and mother; but that is no longer the case; he has now to 'leave his father and mother' and enter into this new relationship. That is a staggering statement, especially in view of the fact that there is so much teaching in the Scripture about the relationship of parents and children. The family is the fundamental unit in life, and so the apostle will go on in the next chapter to say, 'Children, obey your parents in the Lord; for this is right'. But that statement must be taken in the light of this, that when a man gets married he is no longer a child in that sense. He leaves his father and mother, he is now entering into a new unity. He comes out of where he was in order that he may enter into this new unity, this new relationship. He is now the head of a new unit, the head of a new family.

It is very largely at this point that tensions tend to arise most acutely, and difficulties occur, in the married relationship. Obviously in all these matters the biblical statements must be taken in their context, and with reason. We must never become legalistic about these things. Take this statement about a man 'leaving his father and mother'. That does not mean, obviously, that he should never have anything to do with them again. The term is 'let him leave', so we must consider the meaning of 'to leave'. It is a very practical matter, of course, but the important thing is the spiritual understanding of what is involved. Sometimes this is treated, as I say, in a legalistic way, and people become harsh and almost unkind to the father and the mother. That is not the apostle's teaching. But he is concerned about the principle, and this is the thing to which we must pay chief attention. In practice it means that this man has to regard himself henceforth, not primarily as a child of his parents, but as the husband of his wife. All his life he has been regarding himself as the child of his parents, and rightly so. 'Honour thy father and thy mother' is one of the Ten Commandments. But now he has to make a great mental adjustment; he has to think matters through, to assume new responsibilities, and to begin to live in a new way. He is no longer in a position of subservience, he now has become the head of a new family. He must regard himself as such, and he must comport himself as such. The leaving of the father and the mother in reality means this, that he must not allow his father and mother to control him as they have always done hitherto. This is the point at which difficulties arise. For twenty, twenty-five, thirty years, that old relationship has been in existence—father and mother, child. It has become a habit, and one thinks instinctively along those lines. But now this man is married. It is difficult for him—it is even more difficult perhaps for his father and mother—to realize the new situation that has come into being; but the teaching here is that the man must leave his father and mother that he may be joined to his wife. He has to assert and to safeguard his new status, and, as I say, defend it against any interference on the part of his parents. And in his own behaviour, he must no longer act simply and only as he did before, because he is now joined to his wife. He is no longer what he was before. He is what he was before—plus, and that plus creates the difference between the old and the new relationship.

Such is the meaning of this expression, 'leave his father and mother'; he has to assert the new position which has come into being as the result of his marriage. And, of course, when you look at it from the standpoint of the father and mother the situation should be equally clear. They must re-adjust themselves even as their son does. They have to realize that their son's first loyalty now is to his wife, and that he is a very poor specimen of manhood, a very poor husband, and, ultimately, a very poor son if he fails to show that loyalty. They must not interfere in this new married life. They have always commanded their son in the past in various ways, and it was right that they should do so. They must not do so any longer; they must recognize that something entirely new has emerged, and that they must not think of their son any longer simply as their son. He is now married, a new unity has been created, and whatever they do to him they do to his wife at the same time. So obviously they cannot treat him as they treated him formerly. All that is included in this idea of a man leaving his father and his mother in order that he may become joined to his wife. It is really the essence of the apostle's teaching about marriage that all parties involved have to realize that a new unity has come into being. It was not there before, but it is there now. The new husband has to realize that he is not what he was; the new wife has to realize that she also is not what she was in her relationship to her parents. The parents on both sides have to realize that they are not what they were before. Everything is different. There has to be a re-adjustment all along the line because of the new unity that has come into existence as the result of a marriage. 'For this cause shall a man leave his father and mother.'

According to biblical teaching there is nothing more drastic that can happen than this double action—'leaving' and 'joining'. The family is the fundamental unit of our earthly life, yet though the man is still the son of his parents, and though, of course, he still belongs in that general sense to his family, the important thing about him is that he is now the head of a new family, and he must be treated with the dignity that corresponds to the new status. He must think of himself in this way; he must not revert to thinking of himself as he was before; and he must not allow his parents to think of him in that way. 'A man shall leave his father and his mother, and shall be joined unto his wife, and they two shall be one flesh'. The moment we realize this, marriage becomes one of the most momentous, indeed the most momentous thing that ever happens in life. Hence, when you are at a marriage service you should realize that this new unity is coming into being, and that you have to re-adjust your thinking, and henceforth think of the bride and the bridegroom in this new relationship. This new married state now has precedence over every other human relationship. A man leaves his father and mother; so does his wife; and it is as this principle is grasped and put into operation that you get the ideal married state that is outlined here, and you see the difference between Christian and non-Christian marriage. That, then, is the first practical injunction that the apostle gives us.

The second is—'Nevertheless let everyone of you in particular so love his wife, even as himself'. In a sense we have already dealt with the point which the apostle is making, as we were dealing with the man in his relationship to his body, and in regard to his thoughts about his wife. The best comment on the matter is that found in the epistle to the Colossians, chapter three, verse nineteen, where the apostle says, 'Husbands, love your wives, and be not bitter against them'. The negative there helps us to understand the positive in this last verse in the fifth chapter of the Epistle to the Ephesians. The great danger obviously is for the husband to domineer. The emphasis is upon the fact that he is the head, he is the leader, he is in the position of responsibility. That is how God established it at the beginning. So the danger confronting the man always, as the apostle puts it there, is 'to be bitter', which means 'to be harsh'. The antidote is, 'Husbands, let everyone of you in particular so love his wife, even as himself'. You are not harsh to yourself, therefore, do not be harsh to your wife, do not be crushing, do not be domineering.

This statement, when it was written by the apostle, was one of the most astounding that had ever been put on paper. When we read of the pagan view of marriage, and especially the typical attitude of husbands towards wives—and, indeed, not only pagan, but also what you read of in the Old

Testament—we see how revolutionary and transforming the teaching is. Wives were virtually nothing but slaves. The whole notion of polygamy conveys that idea. There is the heroic illustration of women rebelling against that view in the first chapter of the book of Esther, in the case of Vashti, the wife of Ahasuerus. But that was very exceptional. The whole notion was really one of slavery, and so husbands were generally guilty of this harshness, this domineering attitude. The wife was but a vassal, a chattel, as it were. But at once when the Christian message comes in the whole idea is entirely transformed and changed. It is in matters like this that the Christian faith staggered and conquered the ancient world in the first century. Nothing like this had ever been taught before. It was partly as the result of Christian people living this new kind of life that the gospel of our Lord and Saviour spread in that ancient world. This is how Christians testify to the truth of the gospel. The idea that Christians testify by getting up and speaking in a meeting is not found much in the New Testament, if at all. The testimony was borne in their ordinary daily lives. For a man to speak kindly and affectionately to his wife was something that was almost unheard of; and it was as they saw this that people began to ask, What is this? And especially when they saw it in a man who had been very different as a pagan. A new tenderness had come into human life.

True marriage is an illustration of the New Testament teaching about love; it is what you find in 1 Corinthians 13 being put into practice in the married relationship. It was introduced in the eighteenth verse, which is the key to it all: 'Be not drunk with wine, wherein is excess; but be filled with the Spirit'. If you are filled with the Spirit you will be different in every realm and relationship. The apostle is here giving us one illustration of it—the home. That is the place where it should be seen if anywhere; that is the place to judge a man and a woman—in the home, what they are there. Now, says the apostle, let it be known in the home that you are filled with the Spirit, so that anybody who comes to visit you will be staggered, will be taken aback by this, and ask, What is this? There is no greater recommendation to the truth and power of the Christian faith than a Christian husband and wife, Christian marriage, and a Christian home. That helped to revolutionize the ancient world. Remember, then, the second injunction given to the husband. He is given this position of dignity and of leadership and of headship; and if he understands what it means he will never abuse it, he will never misuse it, by being harsh or dictatorial or unkind or unfair. To be guilty of such behaviour is a denial of the marriage principle, and means that there is an absence of the Spirit.

But let us look at the other side. The third injunction is, 'and the wife see that she reverence her husband'. The apostle used a very striking word here. It is rightly translated in the Authorized Version as 'reverence'; but the word really means 'fear'. 'And the wife see that she fears her husband'. But we must remember that there are different types of fear. There is a fear, as John reminds us in his First Epistle (chapter 4) 'that hath torment'. That is not the fear the apostle speaks of here; he speaks of 'reverential' fear. What it really means is 'deference'. 'Wives, see that you treat your husbands with deference', 'with reverential obedience'. Here, again, is an idea the apostle has already introduced when he was dealing with the wives. He says,

> Wives, submit yourselves unto your own husbands, as unto the Lord. For the husband is the head of the wife, even as Christ is the head of the church: and he is the saviour of the body. Therefore as the church is subject unto Christ, so let the wives be to their own husbands in everything.

He comes back to it again here, 'Let the wife see that she treats her husband with due deference, with reverential obedience'.

Perhaps the best commentary on this is found in the First Epistle of Peter, chapter 3 and verse 6, where Peter is in his own way dealing with exactly the same subject. Peter goes back to the great example and pattern of this particular teaching. He puts it in this form: 'Likewise, ye wives, be in subjection to your own husbands'—the same idea, 'deference'—'that if any obey not the word, they also may without the word be won by the conversation of the wives'. Peter here introduces a slightly different matter, to which I will refer in a moment. However, in order to impress this upon the wives, he proceeds to say, 'For after this manner in the old time the holy women also, who trusted in God, adorned themselves, being in subjection unto their own husbands'. Then in the sixth verse, 'Even as Sarah obeyed Abraham, calling him lord: whose daughters ye are, as long as ye do well, and are not afraid with any amazement'. Being interpreted, it means something like this. The wife is to treat her husband with deference; in other words, she is to recognize this biblical and Christian view of marriage, she is to regard the husband as her head, the head of this new unit. They are both one, but there is a head to the unit, as there is a head to our body, as Christ is the head of the church. As the husband is the head, the wife is to treat him with the deference that is becoming in one who realizes that relationship. So what it means for the wife is that the deference which she formerly paid primarily to her parents she is now to pay to her husband. Such is the meaning of the injunction in Psalm 45, verse 10, which puts it like this: 'Forget also thine own people, and thy father's house'. That was addressed prophetically to the Christian church; that is what she is to do when she becomes joined to her heavenly bridegroom; but it is also applicable to the case of the wife in the marriage relationship. 'Forget thine own people, and thy father's house.' As the man is commanded to leave his father and his mother, the wife is to forget her own people and her father's house. I repeat again, that you have to use common sense in interpreting words such as these. She is not to forget in an absolute sense, but she is to forget in this sense, that she is no longer to be controlled by her parents. The man is not to be controlled by his parents, and the wife is not to be controlled by her parents.

It may occur to someone to ask this question: Why, in connection with the plain teaching about marriage, are we told that the man is to leave his father and mother and to be joined unto his wife, while there is no corresponding statement about the woman either in Genesis chapter 2, or in Ephesians chapter 5? The answer, it seems to me, is quite simple. The woman is always in this position of paying deference. The man was in this position until he got married; but from that point onwards he becomes the head. The women pays deference to her parents; she gets married, and now she pays deference to her husband. She is always in the position of paying the deference, she is never the head. But the man who formerly was a child and a son and paid deference now becomes the head and receives this deference from his wife. As we work these things out in detail, is it not obvious, that it is because people have no conception of this teaching that there is so much trouble in marriages, and so many breakdowns?

There is nothing that is so fatal to a marriage as that either partner should be paying deference to a third party. In so doing they are breaking the unity, they are failing to realize the fact of this new unit and the headship of the man in the new unit. So the wife must see to it that she pays this reverential deference to her husband. She has to make a mental and spiritual adjustment as had her husband also in his case. She does not receive her instructions any longer from parents; she does not submit herself to them, she submits herself to her husband. She still maintains the relationship of daughter, of course; but she must see to it that her own attitude is right, and that the attitude of her father and mother is right. So often there is failure at this point on the one side or the other. The man who gets married becomes absorbed into his wife's family, or the wife becomes absorbed into her husband's family. That is wrong on both sides and should never be allowed to happen. This is a new family. The relationships of love should be maintained with the parents on both sides, but never in terms of deference and of submission. And the essence, the whole secret of Christian marriage, and of a happy married life is, that the man and the woman who get married realize this at the beginning, and act upon it, and stand to it at all costs. If there is interference by the parents on either side they are guilty of sin, and of failure to understand and to live according to the biblical teaching concerning marriage. 'Let the wife see that she reverence her husband'. That is the great adjustment she makes. She submits to him. She must not compete with him, she must not strive with him; she must recognize that the essence of marriage is that she pays this deference to him.

There is an odd phrase used by the Apostle Peter, which we must glance at for a moment: 'Even as Sarah', he says, 'obeyed Abraham, calling him lord'. Have you been interested in the change of fashion with respect to this matter? One can read about people in the eighteenth century and notice how the wife habitually referred to her husband as Mr So-and-so. You may smile at that, you may ridicule it, and I will agree with you; but I am quite sure that we have gone too far to the opposite extreme. There is a right balance in these matters. Sarah called Abraham 'lord', and thereby she recognized the biblical principle. Then we read, 'whose daughters ye are, as long as ye do well, and are not afraid with any amazement'. The meaning is this: Christian wives are to pay deference to their husbands, and Peter tells them that they should do so in spite of what the pagan women round about them might say. Here was something new, it was rare, it was exceptional, and of course it created a great stir. When the pagan women, who were restless and rebellious—and rightly so—saw a woman behaving in this manner, offering and paying this deference to her husband, many of them would attack her, and persecute her. What Peter is saying is this: Go on doing it because it is right; do not let them frighten you, do not let their persecution make the slightest difference to you. Let them insult you as much as they like; take no notice of them. Do not be afraid with any amazement. And indeed, even if the husband misunderstands it and abuses it, go on doing it, says the apostle; 'do not be afraid with any amazement'. Do what is right. Do not be worried at what other people may say. This twentieth-century pagan world in which we are living says the same thing still; Christian wives will be told that they are being foolish, that they are denying their rights as women. Do not pay any attention, says Peter, let the people of the world say what they will. What do they understand? They have not got Christian minds, they are not filled with the Spirit. Realize always that you are meant to do that which is right, that which is good; and do not be frightened, do not be put off, do not allow them to interfere with your conduct and your behaviour. Such, then is the apostle's last injunction. We cannot but comment on the wonderful balance which is ever preserved in the Scriptures.

The apostle sums it all up in verse 33, 'Nevertheless, let every one of you in particular so love his wife even as himself, and the wife see that she reverence her husband'. As long as they both do that there is no risk of dispute about 'rights' or about 'my position', or 'my status'. Here is a man given headship; yes, but because he loves his wife as himself he never abuses his position. And here is a woman submitting herself to this great and glorious ideal. She need never be afraid that she will be taken advantage of, or that she will be trodden upon. Husband and wife are both dealt with, and the balance is perfect and entire. We realize, of course, that the Apostle Paul in this statement is writing on the assumption that both the husband and the wife are Christians. The Apostle Peter, as we saw, in his First Epistle, chapter 3, was writing partly on the assumption that the husband might not be a Christian; but everything we have here is on the assumption that both the partners are Christians. And as the apostle does not treat anything else I have refrained from doing so. This is how a Christian man and a Christian woman become married and become this new unit—and I would repeat again that there is no more wonderful way of testifying to the difference it makes to be a Christian than just this.

Surely one of the greatest needs in this modern world of ours is found at this precise point. Most people are troubled about the discord between nations. That is right, and it is also right that we should be deeply concerned about the clashes within nations. People are giving their opinions, and talking boldly, and condemning this side and that side. But when you get to know something about the private lives of some of the people who are most eloquent in that respect, you will find that, in their own married lives, they are doing exactly the same things that they are condemning! How ridiculous it is! One great difference between Christianity and secularism is that secularism is always talking about generalities, and the individual is forgotten. Christianity realizes that the mass, the nation, is nothing after all but a collection of individuals. I have very little interest in what a statesman has to say if he does not carry out his principles in his own personal life. What right has he to talk about the sanctity of international contracts, and to say what people should do and not do in groups, if he is not carrying out in his own private life the precepts he gives to men and women in their various spheres? It is as individuals are put right that a nation is put right. The most glorious epochs in the history of this country have followed times when a personal gospel has been preached, and when a large number of individuals have become Christians. It is only then that we have begun to approximate to a Christian nation. But it is no use telling people to employ Christian principles in their conduct if they are not Christians themselves, and if they do not understand the Christian faith in a personal sense. That is my answer to those who criticize evangelical preaching and biblical exposition, saying, 'I thought you would have had something to say about disarmament conferences, or about what is happening in South Africa, and here you are talking about husbands and wives. I wanted to know how to solve the great world problems'. I trust that by now it is clear that it is evangelical preaching alone which really deals with these big problems, all else is but talk. You can organize marches and make your protests. It all comes to nothing, and makes not the slightest difference to anyone. But if you have a large number of individual Christians in a nation, or in the world, then and only then can you begin to expect Christian conduct on the international and national level. I do not listen to a man who tells me how to solve the world's problems if he cannot solve his own personal problems. If a man's home is in a state of discord, his opinions about the state of the nation or the state of the world are purely theoretical. We can all talk, but the problem is how to apply Christian doctrine in practical living. And it is precisely at this point that you must be 'filled with the Spirit'.

In the light, then, of the several principles which have emerged, we can draw certain conclusions about Christian marriage. First, the importance of 2 Corinthians 6:14: 'Be ye not unequally yoked together with unbelievers'. Having understood something about the true nature of marriage, and of Christian marriage in particular, is it not an obvious deduction? A Christian should not marry a non-Christian; if he does he is asking for trouble. You cannot get the two sides, the balance indicated in this last verse, unless the two partners are Christians. 'Be not unequally yoked together with unbelievers'.

Secondly, there is only one thing that really breaks marriage, and that is, adultery. 'The two shall be one flesh', and it is only when that 'one flesh' is broken that the marriage is broken. According to the biblical teaching—and you will find it in the Sermon on the Mount and elsewhere—there is no cause for divorce and the breaking of a marriage apart from adultery. That is a cause, because it breaks the 'one flesh'.

Thirdly and lastly, the supreme thing always is to consider our Lord Jesus Christ. If a husband and a wife are together considering him, you need have no worry about their relationship to each other. Our human relationships and affections and loves are cemented by our common love to him. If both are living to him and his glory and his praise, if both have got uppermost in their minds the analogy of Christ and the church, and what he has done for the church that she might be redeemed, and that they, as individuals, might become the children of God—if they are overwhelmed by that thought and governed by it, there will be no danger of their personal relationship meeting with disaster. The headship of the husband will be the same kind of headship as the headship of Christ over the church. He gave himself for her; he died for her; he nourishes and cherishes her life; he lives for her; he intercedes for her; his concern is that she may be glorious and spotless and blameless, without spot, or wrinkle, or any such thing. That is the secret—that we are ever to be looking unto him and realizing that marriage is but a pale reflection of the relationship between Christ and his church. So the principle of success in marriage is this: 'Let this mind be in you which was also in Christ Jesus'. 'Husbands, let everyone of you in particular so love his wife even as himself, and the wife see that she reverence her husband'. 'Husbands, love your wives, even as Christ also loved the church, and gave himself for it'. Thank God we are brought into a new life, we are given a new power, and everything is changed—'old things are passed away, behold, all things are become new'. All the relationships of life are transfigured and transformed, are elevated and uplifted, and we are enabled to live after the pattern and the example of the Son of God.

ALSO AVAILABLE FROM
THE BANNER OF TRUTH TRUST

Life in the Spirit in Marriage, Home & Work
D. M. Lloyd-Jones

This is the sixth in a series of eight volumes which comprise Dr Lloyd-Jones' full exposition of the Epistle to the Ephesians, and from which the chapters in *Christian Marriage* were extracted. The sermons were originally preached as part of a long sermon series at Westminster Chapel on Sunday mornings between 1954 and 1962. Since these volumes were first published in the 1970s, many Christians across the world have found great encouragement and direction from their contents. The complete series includes:

God's Ultimate Purpose (Eph. 1:1-23)	*Darkness and Light* (Eph. 4:17-5:17)
God's Way of Reconciliation (Eph. 2:1-22)	*Life in the Spirit* (Eph. 5:18-6:9)
Unsearchable Riches of Christ (Eph. 3:1-21)	*Christian Warfare* (Eph. 6:10-13)
Christian Unity (Eph. 4:1-16)	*Christian Soldier* (Eph. 6:10-20)

ISBN: 978-0-85151-194-8   371pp.   Clothbound

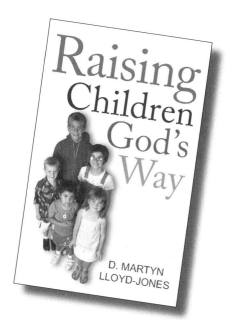

Raising Children God's Way
D. M. Lloyd-Jones

Our age has witnessed an almost total collapse of the family unit, and in many places the majority of children are raised in 'broken homes'. This short book, which comprises five of Dr Lloyd-Jones' Ephesians sermons, will help parents make use of the opportunity to show God's love in this troubled age through their relationship with their children.

If you're looking for a quick-fix solution to temper tantrums or what time to put your eight-year-old to bed, you'll be disappointed. The Doctor is no super-nanny! Neither will you get trendy terminology, current sociological analysis or pop psychology. What you will find is sound biblical teaching and wise counsel from an experienced pastor and teacher, and his words are just as challenging for us now as they were when preached.
[EVANGELICAL TIMES]

ISBN: 978-0-85151-958-6   85pp.   Paperback

About the Publisher

THE Banner of Truth Trust originated in 1957 in London. The founders believed that much of the best literature of historic Christianity had been allowed to fall into oblivion and that, under God, its recovery could well lead not only to a strengthening of the church today but to true revival.

Inter-denominational in vision, this publishing work is now international, and our lists include a number of contemporary authors along with classics from the past. The translation of these books into many languages is encouraged.

A monthly magazine, *The Banner of Truth*, is also published and further information will be gladly supplied by either of the offices below or from our website.

THE BANNER OF TRUTH TRUST

3 Murrayfield Road
Edinburgh, EH12 6EL
UK

PO Box 621, Carlisle
Pennsylvania, 17013
USA

www.banneroftruth.co.uk